My Wee Granny's Meat Free Recipes

Home Style recipes
from my wee granny's table to yours

Angela Hossack

Dedicated to my Wee Granny –
Annie Clark
1890-1971

Also by Angela Hossack

My Wee Granny's Old Scottish Recipes
My Wee Granny's Bannocks and Bakes
My Wee Granny's Soups and Stews
My Wee Granny's Full Table

Copyright © Angela Hossack 2020

The right of Angela Hossack to be identified as author of this work has been asserted in accordance with the Copyright, Designs and Patents Act 1988.

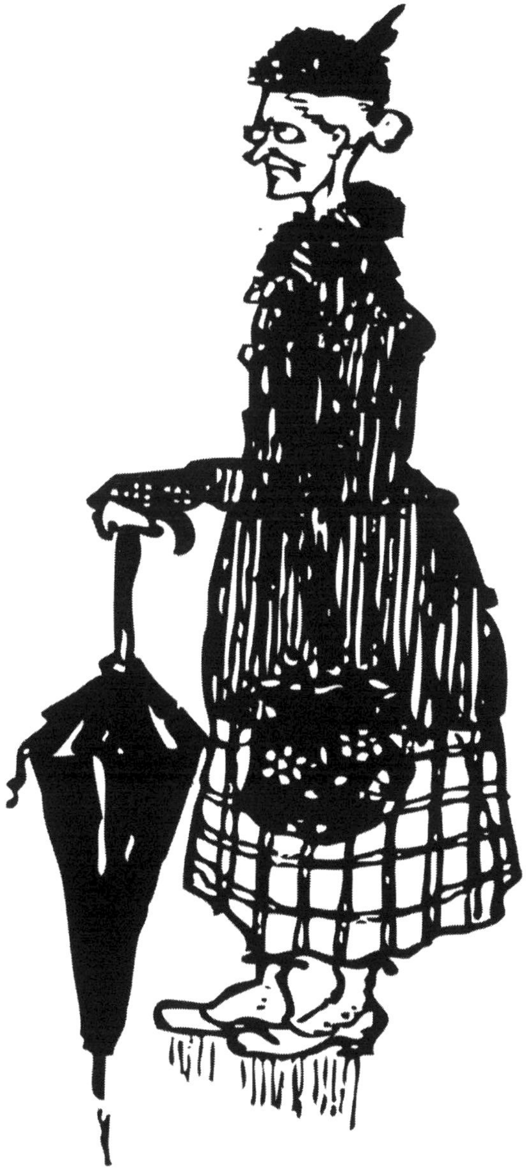

Contents

Introduction

Stocks

Vinaigrettes

Sweet Sauces

Savoury Sauces

Catsups

Syrups, Pickles and Chutney

Eggs

Light Bites

Soups

Stews

Curries

Pasta Dishes

Dishes with Pulses and Beans

Savoury Rice dishes

Fish and Seafood

Introduction

When my wee granny was raising a family of three children in the early part of the twentieth century, the national Scottish larder of game and fish wasn't always affordable, but vegetables, cereals, pulses and beans were always to hand. In my other books of her recipes (*My Wee Granny's Scottish Recipes, My Wee Granny's Soups and Stews, My Wee Granny's Bannocks and Bakes, My Wee Granny's Full Table*) her versatility and ability to cook and bake with limited ingredients, in a simple and delicious way, was reflected across all aspects of the traditional Scottish menu.

Many of her dishes could have ingredients substituted to produce meat free meals, however, I thought I would do her meat free recipes justice and give them a book to themselves.

My wee granny was born at the latter part of the nineteenth century (1890) during a time when Scotland began to have an influx of immigrants from Pakistan, India, the Middle East, and Italy, and some of her recipes are influenced by what she knew these new neighbors cooked. For centuries before, Scottish fare had an element of French influence (Mary Queen of Scots went to France as a child and returned as an adult and brought with her a distinct French taste), and many of today's Scottish recipes continue to be inspired by that past French influence.

Fresh vegetables, cereals, and fish were the foundation of the staple diet she provided for her family, and she always strived to be creative with what she put on the plate.

Across the decades – and, indeed the centuries – these recipes were handed down and used to feed generations of my family. Over time (across five generations) the family has continued to follow and use her recipes, and – at times – added to them.

Enjoy.

Stocks

My wee granny always had a stockpot on the go and, more often than not (especially in lean times) that stockpot was a basic vegetable one. She wasted nothing, and the stockpot was added to - sometimes over days - with peelings, leftover vegetables, the stalks from herbs such as parsley and coriander, and sometimes even fruit.

When fish and shellfish were in abundance, she made a rich fresh stock from the bones, heads and shells.

A good stock was fundamental to many recipes, and my wee granny (as well as almost every woman in Scotland tasked with cooking for large families) depended on it to make their nutritious soups, stews, gravies and sauces. They knew that, without a good stock, the dish had no body.

Those of you, who are as old as I am, may remember when everything we ate seemed to be so much tastier than the food we eat now. One of the reasons could be that more salt and more fat was used. Back in the day, there wasn't the health warnings that we're all now used to hearing about. Today, we're advised to reduce our salt and fat intake. We didn't always know about cholesterol and high blood pressure and the effects of salt and fat on those conditions, but we know now and, so, we have to look to healthier means of seasoning our stocks.

A little salt and a little fat will continue to be used in my wee granny's stock recipes, but other ingredients

– some of which she used and some of which I added to replace the lost salt and fat – have found their way into my stockpots over the years. I've experimented with these ingredients and find that they don't take away from the basic deliciousness of my wee granny's basic stocks.

The most important thing to remember about a good stock is that it needs time… hours and hours of time, but you don't have to stand over it and watch it. You can leave it alone. Just throw your bits and pieces in the pot, cover with water, put a tight lid on and leave it alone for at least four hours, but preferably longer. Your basic **vegetable stock** – scrubbed and chopped carrots with their skins left on, the outside celery stalks that you tend to discard, a couple of whole onions, the outside leaves and the end root of the leek (or a whole leek if you have one going spare), cabbage, broccoli and cauliflower stalks, leftover raw and cooked vegetables and a whole garlic bulb (roasted whole first). Use also any leftover salad tomatoes, spring onions (scallions), sweetcorn, peas and peppers. Put everything in a pot with water (The amount of water will depend on how much bits and pieces you've added to the pot, but you must at least ensure everything is covered by water and then add a further 2 cups), put it on to boil, cover with a tight lid, simmer and forget about it.

When it has simmered for at least four hours, carefully drain through a fine colander, ensuring you squeeze out every last bit of stock and then discard the veggie bits and pieces.

Leave the seasoning until after you have drained and sieved through the colander and, this way, you won't lose any of the seasoning with the discarded vegetables. Season to taste with a little salt, white pepper, celery salt, onion salt and (if preferred, a little garlic paste).

Basic fish stock – fish heads and bones fried for a few minutes gently in butter alongside a roughly chopped onion, 2 stalks of roughly chopped celery and roughly chopped stalks of parsley. Season with celery salt, thyme, a bay leaf, salt and pepper then put in your stock pot, add a cup of white wine to every litre of water and simmer for one hour. Strain through a sieve. For a **richer shellfish stock** use the heads and shells of prawns, lobster shells, razor fish shells and the strained liquor of mussels and follow the method for your basic fish stock but cook out for an additional 30 minutes

Vinaigrettes

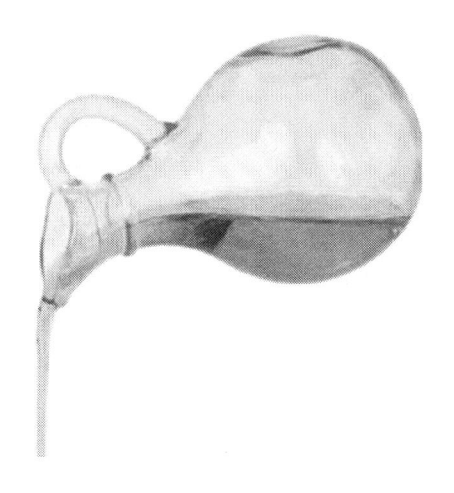

Orange and mint Vinaigrette

<u>What you will need:</u>

The juice of one orange
6 mint leaves
The juice of one lime
4 tablespoons of white wine vinegar
5 tablespoons of extra virgin olive oil
Salt and pepper to season

<u>What you will need to do:</u>

Mix together the orange and lime juice together with the vinegar and add a pinch of salt and pepper
Finely chop the mint and add to the mix
Taste and add more seasoning if required

Lemon and Thyme Vinaigrette

What you will need:

1 unwaxed lemon
A quarter of a cup of lemon juice
Half a cup of extra virgin olive oil
I clove of garlic
Enough freshly chopped thyme leaves to fill one tablespoon
Salt and pepper to season

What you will need to do:

Ensure that the lemon is washed and dried thoroughly
Finely slice and add to a jar
Add the lemon juice and olive oil and mix
Crush the garlic and add
Add the thyme and season with the salt and pepper
Mix thoroughly and add extra seasoning if required

Mustard Vinaigrette (1)

What you will need:

Half a cup of extra virgin olive oil
2 tablespoons of white wine vinegar
1 teaspoon of Dijon mustard
1 clove of garlic
A pinch of smoked paprika
Salt and pepper to taste

What you will need to do:

Mix together the olive oil and the vinegar
Crush the garlic and add to the mix with the mustard and the paprika
Season with the salt and pepper
Mix thoroughly and add seasoning if required

Mustard Vinaigrette (2)

<u>What you will need:</u>

3 tablespoons of extra virgin olive oil
3 tablespoons of corn oil
2 tablespoons of balsamic vinegar
1 teaspoon of Dijon mustard
1 clove of garlic
Half a teaspoon of dried parsley
Salt and pepper to taste

<u>What you will need to do:</u>

Mix together the olive oil, corn oil and the balsamic vinegar
Crush the garlic and add to the mix with the mustard and the parsley
Season with the salt and pepper
Mix thoroughly and add seasoning if required

Herb Vinaigrette

<u>What you will need:</u>

3 tablespoons of extra virgin olive oil
3 tablespoons of vegetable oil
1 bunch of flat-leafed parsley
12 basil leaves
A quarter of a teaspoon of dried oregano
2 cloves of garlic
4 tablespoons of red wine vinegar
1 teaspoon of honey
Salt and pepper

<u>What you will need to do:</u>

mince the garlic
chop the parsley and basil leaves
mix together with the honey and oregano
then mix in the vegetable and olive oil
season with salt and pepper.

Garlic Vinaigrette

What you will need:

2 cloves of garlic
Half a cup of extra virgin olive oil
3 tablespoons of balsamic vinegar
Salt and pepper to taste

What you will need to do:

Grind the garlic into a puree
Add the balsamic vinegar
Whisk he olive oil and add to the mix
Season with salt and pepper
Mix thoroughly

Sweet Sauces

Cherry sauce

What you will need:

2 cups of fresh cherries
2 tablespoons of water
Half a teaspoon of lemon juice
2 tablespoons of sugar
2 teaspoons of corn flour
Pinch of salt

What you will need to do:

Take the stems off the cherries and pit them
Add the cherries to a pan with the water, the salt and the sugar, bring to a gentle simmer, and simmer for 3 or 4 minutes
Mix the cornflour to a paste with a little water and mix through the cherry sauce
Add the lime juice

Apple Sauce

<u>What you will need:</u>

4 apples
1 tablespoon of caster sugar
1 tablespoon of butter

<u>What you will need to do:</u>

Peel and core the apples, then slice

Put the apples in a pan and add the sugar and the butter

Bring to a gentle simmer, cover and simmer for around 15minutes

Caramel Sauce

<u>What you will need:</u>

250 g of caster sugar
1 cup of double cream
1 tablespoon of butter
4 tablespoons of water

<u>What you will need to do:</u>

You need a heavy saucepan or frying pan
Put the sugar in the pan with the water
Slowly bring up the heat until the sugar dissolves and then raise the heat until it is bubbling
Allow it to bubble gently for 4 minutes and then take off the heat
Stir in the cream and butter

Gooseberry Sauce

What you will need:

2 cups of gooseberries
2 tablespoons of caster sugar
1 teaspoon of butter

What you will need to do:

Top and tail the gooseberries
Place the sugar and the butter in a pan and on a low heat, melt and mix
Add the gooseberries
Bring to a gentle simmer, cover and simmer for 10 minutes
Remove the lid, and simmer for a further 5 minutes

Cranberry Sauce

What you will need:

Half a cup of brown sugar
One cup of fresh orange juice
2 cups of fresh cranberries

What you will need to do:

Add the sugar and the orange juice to a pan and bring to a simmer
Stir in the cranberries, bring back to a simmer, and simmer for 5 minutes – ensuring the cranberries hold their shape
(if using frozen cranberries, simmer for a further 2 or 3 minutes

Chocolate Sauce (1)

What you will need:

A large block of dark chocolate (at least 70% solids)
A tablespoon of butter
A cup of double cream
1 tablespoon of caster sugar

What you will need to do:

Break up the chocolate and put it in a bowl
Bring a pan of water to the boil, and reduce to a rolling simmer
place the bowl on top. Stir the chocolate until it melts
place the cream and the butter in another pan and heat then pour in the melted chocolate, stirring until fully combined

Chocolate Sauce (2)

As recipe (1) only replace sugar with 2 tablespoons of golden syrup and, at the end, add one tablespoon of Disaronno liqueur

Savoury Sauces

Basic gravy sauce

<u>What you will need:</u>

1 onion
2 carrots
2 sticks of celery
1 tablespoon of tomato puree
1 bay leaf
One tablespoon of butter
1 tablespoon of sugar
2 tablespoons of flour
2 cups of vegetable stock
1 tablespoon soy sauce

<u>What you will need to do:</u>

Chop the vegetables and then fry in the butter with the bay leaf until the vegetables turn brown
Add the sugar and continue frying until vegetables are completely soft
Add the stock, the tomato puree, and the flour
Stir and simmer for a couple of minutes
Sieve and discard the pulp
Stir through the soy sauce

Brown Butter Sauce (1)

<u>What you will need:</u>

Half a cup of butter
1 clove of garlic
Pinch of black pepper

<u>What you will need to do:</u>

Mince the garlic
Melt the butter in a pan
Add the garlic and the pepper
Over a low heat, stir continuously for about 5 minutes
until the butter begins to turn brown
Remove immediately from the heat

Brown Butter Sauce (2)

<u>What you will need:</u>

Half a cup of butter
1 clove of garlic
1 tablespoon of chopped sage
1 tablespoon of chopped chives
Pinch of black pepper

<u>What you will need to do:</u>

As for recipe (1)
When you remove from the heat, stir in the chopped sage and chopped chives

Cashew Butter Sauce (1)

What you will need:

1 cup of cashew nuts
1 clove of garlic
One teaspoon of extra virgin olive oil
1 shallot
1 teaspoon of lime juice

What you will need to do:

Mince the garlic and finely chop the shallot and add to a frying pan with the oil and the cashew nuts
Fry until the shallots brown
Add the lime juice and blend in a food processor until smooth and creamy

Cashew Butter Sauce (2)

<u>What you will need:</u>

One quarter cup of the cashew butter sauce (recipe 1)
2 tablespoons of water
1 tablespoon reduced salt soy sauce
1 tablespoon of toasted sesame oil
2 teaspoons of maple syrup
1 teaspoon of finely grated ginger
One quarter of a teaspoon of chili flakes

<u>What you will need to do:</u>

Simply blend all the ingredients together

Roasted Tomato Sauce

What you will need:

20 cherry tomatoes
2 cloves of garlic
1 shallot
Quarter of a cup of extra virgin olive oil
salt and pepper

What you will need to do:

Finely chop the garlic and the shallot and add to the olive oil and mix through
Place the tomatoes on a baking tray and drizzle over the olive oil mixture, ensuring every tomato is coated
Roast in a medium oven until the tomatoes turn squishy
Peel off the skins
Blend in a food processor

Mushroom Sauce (1)

<u>What you will need:</u>

2 cups of chopped mushrooms
2 chopped shallots
1 cup of cream
2 tablespoons of butter
Salt and pepper

<u>What you will need to do:</u>

Melt the butter in a pan
Add the shallots and fry for a couple of minutes
Add the chopped mushrooms, the salt and the pepper
Fry for a further 2 minutes and then add the cream
Simmer gently until the cream reduces

Mushroom Sauce (2)

What you will need:

As for recipe (1) but replace the cream with half a cup of vegetable stock and half a cup of milk
3 cloves of chopped garlic
One teaspoon of chopped parsley

What you will need to do:

Melt the butter in a pan
Add the shallots and the garlic and fry for a couple of minutes without burning the garlic
Add the chopped mushrooms, the salt and the pepper
Fry for a further 2 minutes and then add the stock and the milk
Simmer gently until it reduces by half

Two Cheese Sauce

What you will need:

One cup of grated strong cheddar
Half a cup of crumbled blue cheese
2 cups of milk
2 tablespoons of flour
1 tablespoon of butter

What you will need to do:

Add the milk, the flour and the butter to a saucepan
Bring to a gentle simmer, whisking continuously
When thickened
Continue whisking and blend in the cheese until melted through

Onion, Cheese and Parsley Sauce

What you will need:

1 cup of grated strong cheddar
Half a chopped onion
2 tablespoons of butter
2 tablespoons of flour
1 tablespoon of chopped parsley
Salt and pepper

What you will need to do:

Melt the butter in a pan and add the chopped onion
Fry gently until soft without browning the onion
Add the flour and mix through and cook for a minute or so
Gradually add the milk and when it is a thick consistency, add the grated cheese
When melted and well blended, add the parsley and the salt and pepper to taste

Onion Sauce (1)

<u>What you will need:</u>

1 tablespoon of butter
2 tablespoons of flour
One and a half cups of milk
Half a sliced onion
1 teaspoon of chopped parsley
Salt and pepper to taste

<u>What you will need to do:</u>

Melt the butter in a pan and add the flour and stir through
Remove from the heat and slowly add the milk, stirring continuously
Return to the heat and add the sliced onions
Bring to a gentle simmer and simmer for 2 minutes
Add the parsley and salt and pepper to taste

Onion Sauce (2)

What you will need:

2 tablespoons of butter
1 chopped onion
4 teaspoons of caser sugar
2 teaspoons of balsamic vinegar
One cup of white wine
1 cup of vegetable stock
2 tablespoons of flour

What you will need to do:

Melt one of the tablespoons of butter in a pan and add the chopped onions and fry until soft for about 10 minutes
Add the caster sugar and the balsamic vinegar and bring to a boil
Simmer until the mixture reduces and the onions are well browned
Add the white wine, bring to the boil, and reduce by half
Add the vegetable stock
Season with the salt and pepper
Separately, mix the remaining butter with the flour and over a period of 2 to 3 minutes gently blend into the pan to thicken

Onion Sauce (3)

What you will need:

3 tablespoons of butter
2 sliced onions
2 cups of whole milk
2 bay leaves
7 cloves
5 slices of white bread (crustless)
One cup of double cream
Salt and pepper

What you will need to do:

Heat the butter in a pan, add the onions and the bay leaves and fry until the onions are soft but not browned
Add the milk and the cloves and bring to a gentle simmer
Simmer until reduced by half
Remove the bay leaves and the cloves and break in 3 slices of the bread to the mix
Blend in a food processor
Add the cream and mix in the remaining bread

Pesto Sauce

<u>What you will need:</u>

1 cup of chopped fresh basil
3 cloves of minced garlic
3 tablespoons of pine nuts
one third of a cup of grated parmesan
one third of a cup of extra virgin olive oil
salt and pepper to taste

<u>What you will need to do:</u>

Blend the basil, garlic, pine nuts, and parmesan in a food processor. Add salt and pepper to taste
Add the olive oil gradually to the mix whilst the food processor is running

Egg Sauce

What you will need:

2 eggs
2 tablespoons of cornflour
2 cups of cold milk
1 tablespoon of butter
Salt and pepper – quarter of a teaspoon of each or to taste)
half a teaspoon of lemon juice
2 teaspoons of chopped dill

What you will need to do:

Hard boil the eggs and chop
Mix the cornflour in the milk
Add to a pan and add the butter, salt and pepper to taste
Bring to a gentle simmer, stirring continuously for about a minute
Add the lemon juice, the dill and the eggs

Curry Sauce (1)

<u>What you will need:</u>

1 tablespoon of coconut oil
2 diced onions
4 cloves of minced garlic
1 tablespoon of grated fresh ginger
1 cup of vegetable stock
2 cans of coconut milk
Half a teaspoon each of – cumin, smoked paprika, turmeric, chili powder
2 tablespoons of flour

<u>What you will need to do:</u>

Fry the onions and the garlic in the coconut oil until soft and then add the ginger and the spices. Mix thoroughly and blend in the flour
Add the vegetable stock and the coconut milk
Bring to a gentle simmer and simmer until reduced by half

Curry Sauce (2)

What you will need:

1 tablespoon of butter
2 onions
4 crushed cloves of garlic
1 star anise
1 tablespoon of raisins
I teaspoon of grated ginger
2 cups of vegetable stock
1 teaspoon of lemon juice
2 tablespoons of corn flour
1 teaspoon of turmeric
1 teaspoon of cumin
1 teaspoon of garam masala
1 teaspoon of mild curry powder
Half a teaspoon of black pepper
salt to taste

What you will need to do:

Fry the onions, the ginger and the garlic in the butter until soft but not browned
Stir in the, cumin, garam masala, curry powder, black pepper, raisins and star anise
Fry for a minute and then add the vegetable stock
Simmer gently for 30 minutes, stirring frequently

Remove the star anise

Mix the cornflour with water and add to the sauce and stir until the mixture thickens

Put in a food processor and blend

Add the lemon juice and salt to taste

Curry Sauce (3)

<u>What you will need:</u>

2 tablespoons of coconut oil
1 chopped onion
1 teaspoon grated ginger
4 tomatoes
1 teaspoon of tomato puree
2 teaspoons of curry powder
I can of coconut milk
1 finely chopped red chili
3 cloves of chopped garlic
3 tablespoons of ground almonds
Salt to taste

<u>What you will need to do:</u>

Roast and skin the tomatoes with one of the tablespoons of coconut oil
Fry the onions, garlic, ginger and chili in the coconut oil until soft but not browned
Mix in the curry powder and cook for a minute
Add the skinned tomatoes. the tomato puree and the coconut milk and then stir in the almonds
Bring to a gentle simmer and the remove from the heat
Use a blender to mix to a smooth consistency

White Sauce

<u>What you will need</u>:

1 1/2 tablespoons of butter
1 garlic clove
1 1/2 tablespoons of flour
1 1/2 cups of milk
Salt and pepper to taste

<u>What you will need to do</u>:

Finely chop the garlic then add to a pan with the butter. Fry gently for a minute and mix in the flour. Lower the heat.
Stirring continuously, gently add the milk and continue vigorously stirring until the sauce begins to thicken then remove from the heat and continue to stir until the sauce completely thickens

Catsups

Walnut Catsup

You need to make it in advance and keep in an airtight jar.
Ensure that your walnuts are not too hard.

To prepare before cooking - take 50 walnuts and squeeze them a little to bruise them and put in a jar with 1 tablespoon of salt and half a litre of vinegar. You then need to allow to marinade for at least a week.
Once marinated, put them in a pot with a teaspoon of nutmeg, a teaspoon of cloves, a teaspoon of ginger a teaspoon of black peppercorns a cm of horseradish 10 small shallots, 200g of anchovies and 250mls (half a pint) of port.

Boil and simmer for half an hour. Taste and add more vinegar or wine if required.

You can either strain and then use the liquid or use the catsup without straining. Store in an airtight jar or bottle.

Liquid Mushroom Catsup

<u>What you will need:</u>

900g (2lbs) of chestnut mushrooms
2 teaspoons of salt
2 bay leaves
1 chopped onion
the zest of 1 lemon
a quarter of a teaspoon of Allspice
a quarter of a teaspoon of cayenne pepper
1 tablespoon of horseradish that has been finely grated
a quarter of a teaspoon of cloves
half a cup of cider vinegar.

<u>What you will need to do:</u>

Carefully wipe and chop the mushrooms then put in a bowl with the salt and the bay leaves, mash them slightly with a potato masher, pat the mixture flat, cover and leave overnight to draw out the liquid.

The next day, add the chopped onion, the lemon zest, the horseradish, the Allspice, the cloves and the cayenne pepper. Stir in the cider vinegar.

Bring to the boil and simmer for 20 minutes.

Strain all the juice and put the liquid mushroom catsup it in an airtight jar or bottle.

Cucumber Catsup

<u>What you will need:</u>

6 cucumbers
4 chopped onions
2 teaspoons of salt
Teaspoon of chopped horseradish
Peel of one lemon
A quarter of a teaspoon of cayenne pepper
A quarter of a teaspoon of black pepper
2 teaspoons of brandy

<u>What you will need to do:</u>

Slice the cucumbers, put in a large bowl and mix through the chopped onions. Add the salt.
Cover and leave to sit for 36 hours.
Strain and add the chopped horseradish, the peel of the lemon, the black pepper and the cayenne pepper.
Bring to the boil and simmer for 15 minutes.
Strain once more
Add 2 teaspoons of brandy

Spicy Tomato Catsup

<u>What you will need:</u>

12 plum tomatoes
1 bay leaf
1 cinnamon stick
One teaspoon of celery salt
Half a teaspoon of chili flakes
I cup of apple cider vinegar
1 onion
1 tablespoon of sugar
2 garlic cloves
A quarter of a teaspoon of allspice
Half a teaspoon of salt

<u>What you will need to do:</u>

Cut the tomatoes in half
Chop the onion
Mince the garlic
In a large pot, add the tomatoes, vinegar, salt, celery salt, sugar, onion, chili flakes, garlic and allspice
Bring to a simmer, cover and simmer for 30 minutes
Puree the mixture and strain to remove skin and seeds
Return to the heat and simmer until thick

Mixed Vegetable Catsup

<u>What you will need:</u>

Half a butternut squash
1 large potato
2 large carrots
1 onion
2 cloves of garlic
Half a teaspoon of dried ginger
A quarter of a teaspoon of garam masala
A half a teaspoon of salt
A teaspoon of chili flakes
2 tablespoons of sugar

<u>What you will need to do:</u>

Peel and chop the vegetables into small pieces
Mince the garlic
Add to a large pot and add the ginger, garlic, chilli flakes, garam masala
Cover with water, bring to a simmer, cover and cook until tender
Strain and mash
Add the sugar and simmer until thick

Syrups, Pickles and Chutneys

Before we get into recipes for pickles and chutneys, - a word about **sweet, and sour pickling mixtures and syrups…**

My wee granny added one of a selection of syrups at the end of the process for most chutneys and used the basic pickling mixture for all pickles.

Vinegar loses its strength when boiled, so only bring to a scalding boil and remove from the heat

What you will need:

Basic rich sweet spiced pickle
1 pint of cider vinegar to 1,5kg of sugar
4 whole cloves, 2-inch cinnamon stick, teaspoon of whole black peppercorns, teaspoon of mace, 2 teaspoons of mustard seeds, 2 crushed bay leaves. 1 tablespoon of whole allspice, 2 teaspoons of coriander seeds - wrapped and tied in cheesecloth

Basic rich sour spiced pickle
Ingredients as for sweet pickle but without the sugar

Pomegranate (Grenadine)
1 cup of unsweetened pomegranate juice, one cup of sugar, orange and lemon peel

Raspberry
2 cups of raspberries, 1 cup of sugar, orange and lemon peel

Cranberry
1 cup of unsweetened cranberry juice, 1 cup of sugar, orange and lemon peel.

What you will need to do:

Simply – add all your selection of ingredients to a pan and bring to a rapid boil, then reduce to a gentle simmer until the mixture reduces and thickens slightly (no more than 5 minutes)
For the pickling mixture, add the spice bag
For the raspberry mixture – strain
Remove the peel.

Sweet Pickled Red Cabbage

What you will need:

2 red cabbages
Salt
1 pint of the sweet pickle mix

What you will need to do:

Slice and layer the cabbage, sprinkling each layer with salt
Cover and put in the fridge overnight
Next day, remove the brine
Put in a pot with 1 pint of the pickling mixture
Bring to the boil and immediately remove from the heat

Pickled White Cabbage

<u>What you will need</u>:

1 large white cabbage
Salt and pepper
1 pint of the sour pickle mix

<u>What you will need to do:</u>

Slice the cabbage and put in a pan. Cover with boiling water and allow to cool
When cold, drain off the water and season with the salt and pepper
Add the sour pickling mix

Pickled Cauliflower

What you will need:

12 cauliflower florets
1 tablespoon of Dijon mustard
2 cups of sweet pickle mix

What you will need to do:

Part boil the cauliflower in salted water for 10 minutes
Drain and allow to cool
When cold, add the mustard to the sweet pickle mix and pour over the cauliflower

Cucumber Pickles

What you will need:

6 cucumbers (2 or 3 inches long)
3 tablespoons of the pickling spice (those spices used for the pickling mix)
1 pint of cider vinegar

What you will need to do:

Slice the cucumbers and put a layer in the bottom of a sealable jar
Sprinkle on some of the pickling spice mixture
Continue layering this way, then cover with the cider vinegar
Seal and leave for at least 4 weeks

Mixed Vegetable Pickle

What you will need:

6 cauliflower florets
¼ of a white cabbage
2 small cucumbers
1 carrot
1 stick of celery
1 red pepper
1 green pepper
6 green string beans

What you will need to do:

Chop the vegetables, cover with salted boiling water, allow to cool overnight
Drain and cover with sweet picking mix

Red Onion chutney

<u>What you will need:</u>

8 red onions
Half a cup of caster sugar
Half a cup of red wine vinegar
Half a cup of red wine
Dash of syrup

<u>What you will need to do:</u>

Peel and slice the onions and add to a pan with the sugar. Bring to a gentle simmer and cook until soft (about 10 minutes)

Add the vinegar and the red wine and continue simmering until the mixture has reduced to a sticky consistency.

Remove from the heat and add the dash of syrup

Tomato chutney (1)

<u>What you will need:</u>

8 ripe tomatoes
3 onions
2 cloves of garlic
I cup of red wine vinegar
1 cup of soft brown sugar
1 teaspoon of dried ground ginger

<u>What you will need to do:</u>

Cut the tomatoes into quarters
Peel and chop the onions
Peel and crush the garlic
Add all ingredients to a heavy pan and bring to a gentle simmer. Cover and simmer for 90 minutes, stirring occasionally, until thick and sticky. Add a dash of syrup.

Tomato chutney (2)

What you will need:

8 ripe tomatoes
3 onions
2 red peppers
2 cloves of garlic
I cup of red wine vinegar
1 cup of soft brown sugar
1 teaspoon of dried ground ginger
Half a teaspoon of smoked paprika
2 tablespoons of sultanas

What you will need to do:

Cut the tomatoes into quarters
Peel and chop the onions
Peel and crush the garlic
Deseed and chop the peppers
Add all ingredients (except the sultanas) to a heavy pan and bring to a gentle simmer. Cover and simmer for 90 minutes, stirring occasionally, until thick and sticky.
Add the sultanas and a dash of syrup

Pineapple chutney (1)

What you will need:

2 pineapples
3 red onions
1 red chili
1 tablespoon of black onion (Nigella) seeds
1 teaspoon turmeric
1 teaspoon of dried ginger
1 cup of soft brown sugar
1 tablespoon of yellow mustard seeds
¾ cup of cider vinegar
1 teaspoon of salt
2 teaspoons of vegetable oil

What you will need to do:

Peel, chop and core the pineapple
Peel and chop the onions and finely chop and de-seed the chili
Add the chopped onions, the chili, onion seeds, mustard seeds, turmeric, ginger and salt to a heavy pan with the oil and fry off until onions are soft
Add the sugar, vinegar, pineapple chunks and simmer for one hour until thick and sticky.

Pineapple chutney (2)

<u>What you will need:</u>

1 pineapple
2 Bramley apples
1 cup of chopped (ready to eat) figs
1 red onions
1 tablespoon of black onion (Nigella) seeds
½ teaspoon of freshly grated nutmeg
1 teaspoon of dried ginger
1 cup of soft brown sugar
1 tablespoon of black mustard seeds
1 cup of cider vinegar
2 teaspoons of salt

<u>What you will need to do:</u>

Peel, chop and core the pineapple and the Bramley apples
Peel and chop the onion
Add all the ingredients (except the sugar) into a heavy pan and bring to a gentle simmer. Simmer until apples are softened.
Add the sugar, mix thoroughly, and simmer for a further 25 minutes until the mixture is thick.

Beetroot Chutney

What you will need:

8 medium raw beetroots
2 Bramley apples
1 red onion
¼ pint of cider vinegar
Zest of 2 unwaxed lemons
The juice of three lemons
2 cups of sugar
¼ teaspoon of salt
¼ teaspoon of black pepper
2 teaspoons of fennel seeds
1 tablespoon of caper berries

What you will need to do:

Cook the beetroot in simmering water its skin until soft, then peel and chop
Peel, core and chop the apples
Peel and chop the onion
Put everything (except the sugar, the capers, and the cooked beetroot) in a heavy pan and bring to a gentle simmer for 10 minutes.
Add the beetroot and mix through, then add the sugar and simmer for a further 20 minutes
Add the capers at the end.

Rhubarb Chutney (1)

What you will need:

6 stalks of rhubarb
1 cup of cider vinegar
1 cup of caster sugar
1 teaspoon of grated ginger
1 cardamom pod
pinch of salt
Pinch of black pepper

What you will need to do:

Melt the sugar in the vinegar in a heavy pot by bringing to a gentle simmer and stirring
Chop the rhubarb and add to the pan along with the ginger and the cardamom pod
Simmer for 20 minutes until rhubarb is soft
Season with salt and pepper

Rhubarb Chutney (2)

Follow recipe for **(1)** only add 1 cup of chopped dates during the cooking of the rhubarb, and then one tablespoon of sultanas at the end

Courgette Chutney

What you will need:

4 medium courgettes
3 medium cooking apples
3 onions
1 cup of sultanas
2 teaspoons chilli flakes
1 teaspoon of grated ginger
1 teaspoon salt
1 cup of sweet pickling mix

What you will need to do:

Dice the courgettes into fairly small pieces and add to a large saucepan.
Peel, core and dice the apples and add to the pan.
Peel and dice the onions and add to your pan.
Add the sultanas, chilli flakes, sea salt and grated ginger to the pan
Make your spice bag by tying up the spices in a large muslin square or ready-made bag and add to the pan.
Cover with the pickling mix and bring slowly to the boil, stirring occasionally
Remove when the mixture reaches the boil.

Eggs

Not everyone can boil, poach, or scramble an egg to perfection, so I'll start with how my wee granny did it, and add in another few of her recipes for eggs

Soft Boiled

Put the eggs into a pan and cover them with boiling water. Let them gently simmer (not really boil) for 10 minutes. Keep the water at no more than 82 degrees

Hard Boiled

Leave the eggs in the simmering water for 25 minutes.

Poached

Break the eggs separately into a cup and let them slide gently into boiling water that has a dash of vinegar or a few drops of lemon juice in it. When the white loses its translucency, the egg is ready

Scrambled

For every egg allow a level teaspoon of melted butter and a tablespoon of milk. Melt the butter in the milk and, when hot, stir in the eggs (do not beat the eggs beforehand) and stir. Scrape from the bottom and mix. Take off as soon as they begin to cook through as the eggs continue cooking for half a minute after they're taken from the pan.

Curried Eggs (1)

What you will need:

6 hard-boiled eggs
curry sauce of your choosing (see curry sauce recipes)

What you will need to do:

Heat the curry sauce
Halve the eggs and place in a dish and cover in the sauce

Curried Eggs (2)

<u>What you will need:</u>

4 eggs
Tablespoon of butter
1 spring onion
½ a teaspoon of chili flakes
½ a teaspoon of turmeric
½ a teaspoon of curry powder

<u>What you will need to do:</u>

Finely chop the spring onion
Beat the eggs and add the chili flakes, turmeric and curry powder
Heat the butter in a pan and add the egg mixture
Fry until very firm and remove from the pan
Chop up and add the spring onion

Deviled eggs

What you will need:

6 hard-boiled eggs
1 teaspoon of Dijon mustard
teaspoon of butter
½ a teaspoon of sugar
Dash of vinegar
Pinch of salt

What you will need to do:

Cut the eggs lengthwise
Scoop out the yolks and mash them, mixing in the other ingredients
Spoon back inside the whites

Savory Omelet

Use the filling of your choice – cheese, sardines, asparagus, mushrooms, prawns – the list is endless

Cook just before serving. Brown and don't overcook. Ensure the pan is hot
Moisten the bottom of the pan with a little butter
Beat the eggs with a little salt and pepper and pour sufficient quantity into the pan. Add whatever filling you want
When the bottom has browned, flip over one half on top of the other. Flip once and serve

Sweet Omlette

Add 1 teaspoon of sugar for each egg used
Cook as for savory omelet and use jam or any other preserve as a filling
Serve with sugar sprinkled on top

Omlette Souffle

Beat the yolks of 6 eggs with 6 tablespoons of caster sugar. Flavour with vanilla or lemon. Whisk the whites to a stiff froth and fold gently and quickly into the yolks
Bake in enameled ramakins in a moderately hot oven for 10 minutes
Serve immediately

Eggs on rice

<u>What you will need:</u>

4 cups of seasoned, cooked rice
4 eggs
8 nobs of butter
Salt

<u>What you will need to do:</u>

Butter an oven-proof dish and put in the cooked rice
Make 4 depressions and break an egg into each depression
Strew the nobs of butter across the top and season with salt
Bake in a moderate oven until the eggs are cooked

Egg and Vegetable Bake

What you will need:

4 potatoes
2 red onions
2 cloves of garlic
2 carrots
1 cup of frozen garden peas
Small tin of sweetcorn
1 courgette
1 cup of grated cheddar cheese
4 eggs
1 tablespoon of extra virgin olive oil
Salt and pepper to taste

What you will need to do:

Peel and dice the potatoes
Peel and chop the onions, and the carrots
Trim the courgetti and cut into ribbons
Chop the garlic
In an oven-proof frying pan fry the potatoes in the oil until they are browned and then add all the other vegetables and the garlic
Cook for 15 minutes
Season with the salt and pepper
Add the courgetti ribbons and the cheese

Make 4 indentations in the mix and break in the eggs
Bake for 10 – 15 minutes (depending on how you want the yolks cooked) in a pre-heated moderate oven

Vegetarian Scotch Eggs

What you will need:

8 eggs
1½ cups red lentils
1 tablespoon of oil
1 onion
2 cloves garlic
1 cup of grated cheddar cheese
6 large pieces sun-dried tomato
1 tablespoon of chopped fresh parsley
2 slices bread
Salt and black pepper
Flour for rolling
Another 3 eggs, lightly beaten
4 sundried tomatoes
2 cups of breadcrumbs
Oil for frying

What you will need to do:

Boil the eggs for 8 minutes, cool under cold water and peel
Cook the red lentils in salted water until tender then drain off excess water
Dice the onion and mince the garlic and fry in the oil until the onions are soft

In a food processor, blend the lentils with the cooked onion and garlic.

Add the grated cheddar cheese, sun-dried tomatoes, parsley, and breadcrumbs. Season with a generous pinch of salt and pepper, and blitz until fairly smooth. Split the mixture into 8 equal portions and form each portion around the boiled eggs

Dip each one in beaten egg, then roll in breadcrumbs. Deep fry the Scotch eggs until the breadcrumbs are golden brown and crispy

Light Bites

Spicy Cauliflower Fritters

<u>What you will need:</u>

1 small cauliflower cut into florets
60g of plain flour
1 shallot
1 clove of garlic
Half a teaspoon of turmeric
1 red chili
Salt and pepper
2 eggs
Vegetable oil (for your deep-fat fryer)

<u>What you need to do:</u>

Finely dice the shallot and mince the garlic
De-seed and finely chop the chili
Put the flour, turmeric, chili, garlic and shallot into a bowl and mix thoroughly. Season with salt and pepper, beat the eggs and add to the mix – ensuring the mixture is well combined. Put to the side
Add the cauliflower florets to slightly salted boiling water and simmer for approximately 3 or 4 minutes, drain and plunge into iced water. When cool, drain and add to the bowl with the other ingredients and gently mix.

Use a tablespoon to place the mixture carefully into the pre-heated vegetable oil (you should get approximately 12 separate fritters from the mix) and fry until golden.

Goat's Cheese and Red Pepper Tartlet

What you will need:

4 red bell peppers
2 tablespoons of olive oil
180g of goat's cheese
2 tablespoons of cream
1 egg yolk
Cold water (enough to combine the pastry)
50g of butter
100g of plain flour
Baking beans and greaseproof paper

What you need to do:

Rub the olive oil onto the peppers and roast in a hot oven for 15 minutes. Remove the seeds and roughly chop.

Make the pastry by rubbing the butter into the flour to make a breadcrumb consistency, then add the water to combine. Chill in the fridge in clingfilm for 30 minutes.

Once chilled, split the dough into 4 equal parts, roll out and line 4 4-inch tart tins. Put greaseproof paper on top of the pastry and add the baking beans.

Bake in a hot oven (200 degrees C) for 10 minutes. Remove the beans and paper and return to the oven for a further 5 minutes. Allow to cool.

Mix the goat's cheese with the cream and the egg yolk and season with salt and pepper.

Divide the peppers amongst the 4 pastry cases. Spoon the goat's cheese on top and return to the oven for approximately 8 minutes.

Roasted Vegetable and Cheddar Cheese Tartlet

What you will need:

2 red onions
2 yellow bell peppers
2 red bell peppers
1 clove of garlic
4 button mushrooms
2 tablespoons of olive oil
200g of grated cheddar cheese

What you need to do:

Roughly chop the onions
Quarter the peppers and remove the seeds
Finely chop/dice the mushrooms
Finely chop the garlic
Mix everything through the olive oil and place in a roasting tin. Put in a hot oven for 15 minutes
Follow the previous recipe to make the pastry tarts
Divide the roasted vegetables amongst 4 pastry shells and top with the grated cheese. Return to the oven for approximately 5 minutes.

Seared Scallops with Quail's Egg

What you will need:

12 scallops
4 quail's eggs
2 tablespoons of butter
Salt and pepper

What you need to do:

Fry the scallops (see previous recipe) in 1 tablespoon of butter
In another small, non-stick, frying pan, fry the quail's eggs leaving the yolks runny
Serve 3 scallops with a quail's egg on top per portion
Season with salt and pepper to taste

Cheese Scallop

What you will need:

1 cup of fresh breadcrumbs
½ a cup of milk
1 tablespoon of butter
2 cups of grated cheese
½ teaspoon of salt
¼ teaspoon of black pepper
2 eggs

What you will need to do:

Add the breadcrumbs to the milk and heat through in a pan. When hot and smooth, add the butter and the cheese. Season with the salt and pepper
Stir and simmer for a minute
Separate the eggs. Whisk the whites to firm peaks
Beat the yolks and add to the mix in the pan and then gently fold in the whites
Place in a buttered baking dish and bake for 15 to 20 minutes in a moderate oven

Scottish Rarebit

What you will need:

4 slices of white bread
¼ cup of butter
1/3 cup flour
1 cup of strong Scottish stout
1 tablespoon of whisky
1 teaspoon of mustard powder
2 cups of grated cheddar cheese
1 teaspoon of Worcester sauce
½ a teaspoon of white pepper
A couple of pinches of salt
Extra butter

What you will need to do:

Melt butter in a small pan and whisk in the flour until it forms a paste. Stir and cook it out for a couple of minutes and then slowly stir in the stout and the whisky.
When you have a smooth sauce, add the mustard powder and the grated cheese. When the cheese is melted, add in Worcestershire sauce and season with salt and pepper.

Toast the bread and then butter it. Heap some of the mixture onto each slice and brown under a pre-heated grill.

Cheesy Potato Turnovers

What you will need:

A bowl of hot mashed potato (quantity to suit)
2 cups of grated cheddar cheese
Teaspoon of salt
½ teaspoon of white pepper
Teaspoon of Dijon mustard
2 eggs
Half a cup of flour
Butter for frying

What you will need to do:

Beat the eggs and mix through the mashed potatoes
Add the salt, pepper and mustard and mix thoroughly
Mix in half of the flour (the other half to use to dredge
Roll out the potato mix, dredging with flour to prevent it sticking
Cut into rounds
Place some cheese in the middle and fold over, nipping the edges closed
Fry in butter until both sides are golden brown

Tomato Croutes

<u>What you will need:</u>

20 cherry tomatoes
4 slices of white bread
Butter
Salt and pepper
Tablespoon of extra virgin olive oil

<u>What you will need to do:</u>

Scald and peel the tomatoes
Butter the bread and arrange in a buttered baking dish
Slice each tomato into 3 and layer onto the bread
Season with salt and pepper
Sprinkle on the olive oil
Bake for half an hour in a moderate oven

Fried Green Tomatoes

What you will need:

4 large green tomatoes
Cup of flour seasoned with salt and pepper
Tablespoon of butter for frying.
What you will need to do:

Slice the tomatoes into ½ inch rounds (discard both ends)
Dust in the seasoned flour and fry until golden brown in the butter
Add more salt and pepper to taste

Soups

Kale and Oatmeal Soup

Serves 4

What you will need:

1 litre of vegetable stock
4 cups (chopped) Green kale (240g)
Quarter of a cup of oatmeal (32g)
Half a cup (150ml) double cream

What you need to do:

Wash and de-vein the kale and roughly chop
Bring your vegetable stock to the boil
Add the kale to the stock and simmer for one hour
Remove the kale and chop up finely and toss it in the oatmeal
Return to the pot
Gently warm the cream and add to the pot
Stir and simmer for 5 minutes

Red Lentil and Barley Soup

Serves 6

What you will need:

1.5 litres of vegetable
1 cup (128g) of red lentils
1 cup pearl barley
4 carrots
1 onion
2 stalks of celery
2 teaspoons of chopped curly leaf parsley

What you will need to do:

Soak the pearl barley in cold water in the fridge overnight.
Rinse the red lentils and the barley and add to the stock. Bring to the boil, cover with a tight lid and begin simmering.
Peel, chop and dice the carrots and onion and add to the pot.
Remove the fibrous stringy bits from the celery and chop into small pieces and add to the pot and gently simmer for one hour.
Add the parsley just before serving

Tattie (Potato) Soup

Serves 6-8

What you will need:

1.5 litres of vegetable stock
2lb (907g) of potatoes
2 onions
2 stalks of celery
Half a pint (250mls) of milk
Cup of curly leaf parsley
Tablespoon of flour
Splash of vegetable oil

What you will need to do:

Chop and dice the potatoes and onions, remove the fibrous stringy bits of the celery and chop into small pieces. Fry all these vegetables in the vegetable oil for 5 minutes.
Bring the stock to the boil and add the vegetables. Cover and simmer for 15 minutes then use a potato masher to mash.
Wash and chop the parsley.
Blend the flour with the milk and add to the pot to thicken. Stir well and add the parsley.

Tattie (Potato) and Leek Soup

Serves 6-8

What you will need:

1.5 litres of vegetable stock
2lb (907g) potatoes
4 carrots
Small swede
2 leeks
Cup of curly leaf parsley

What you need to do:

Dice the potatoes, swede and 3 of the 4 carrots and add to the vegetable stock. Bring to the boil and simmer for 30 minutes.

Wash and cut the leek lengthways and then into small pieces and after the vegetables have simmered for 30 minutes, add the leek to the pot and simmer for a further 30 minutes.

Chop the curly leaf parsley and add it 5 minutes before serving.

Haricot Bean Soup

Serves 6-8

What you will need:

1.5 litres of vegetable stock
340g (12oz) of pre-soaked haricot beans
2 onions
1 swede
450g (1lb) potatoes
1 tablespoon of flour
2 cups of milk
Half a cup of curly leaf parsley

What you will need to do:

Cut and dice the onions, swede and potatoes. Rinse the beans and add to the stock along with the diced vegetables. Bring to the boil and cover with a tight lid. Simmer for 2 hours then force through a sieve and return to the pot. Mix the flour with a little of the milk and stir through the soup to thicken and then add the remaining milk.
Chop the parsley and just before serving, add to the pot.

Tomato Soup

Serves 4

<u>What you will need</u>:

1 litre of vegetable stock
8 large or 10 medium blanched and skinned tomatoes
1 carrot
1 onion
2 tablespoons of sago
2 cups of milk

<u>What you will need to do:</u>

Cut up tomatoes, onion and carrot and add to the stock in a pot. Bring to the boil and add the sago. Simmer for 30 minutes.

Pass through a sieve, return to the pot and add the milk. Stir and heat, but do not boil.

Tomato, red pepper and lentil soup

Serves 4

<u>What you will need</u>:

1 litre of vegetable stock
6 medium blanched and skinned tomatoes
2 red peppers
1 onion
2 cloves of garlic
2 teaspoons of olive oil
Half a cup (60g) of red lentils

<u>What you will need to do</u>:

Quarter the tomatoes, peppers and onion and put on a baking tray with the garlic

Mix the vegetables with the olive oil and roast in a medium oven for 15-20 minutes

Squeeze the roasted garlic from their skins and mix through the roasted vegetables. Remove the pepper skins

Rinse the lentils and add to the stock, bring to a simmer and simmer for 15 minutes, stirring occasionally

Add the vegetables and simmer for a further 10 minutes

Cream of mushroom soup

Serves 4

What you will need:

1 litre of vegetable stock
500g of mixed mushrooms
50g of butter
1 onion
1 cup of crème fraiche
2 tablespoons of cream

What you will need to do:

Chop the mushrooms and the onion and fry in the butter until soft
Add to the stock and bring to a simmer then simmer for 20 minutes
Stir in the crème fraiche and simmer for a further 5 minutes
Blend (blitz) the soup and serve topped with a swirl of cream

Spicy parsnip soup

Serves 4

What you will need:

1 litre of vegetable stock
1 cup of cream
Half a teaspoon of smoked paprika
Half a teaspoon of cumin
Half a teaspoon of chopped ginger
A quarter of a teaspoon of chili powder
6 large parsnips
1 onion
2 cloves of garlic
Knob of butter
Handful of coriander leaves

What you will need to do:

Peel and chop the parsnips and slice the garlic
Add to the butter in a frying pan and fry gently for a few minutes then add the chopped parsnip, the smoked paprika, cumin and chili powder
Fry gently for a few minutes then add to the vegetable stock and simmer for 30 minutes then stir in most of the cream

Blend (blitz) thoroughly until smooth and serve with a swirl of cream and with a garnish of chopped coriander leaves

y vegetable soup

Serves 4

What you will need:

1 litre of vegetable stock (you may need to add more later)
1 cup of milk
2 carrots
2 potatoes
2 small white turnips
1 parsnip
Half a cup of green lentils
1 onion
Half a teaspoon of cumin
Half a teaspoon of smoked paprika
Half a teaspoon of chili powder
Knob of butter

What you will need to do:

Peel and chop all the vegetables and fry off with the knob of butter then add to the vegetable stock and bring to a simmer. Add the spices and then simmer for 15 minutes

Rinse and then add the lentils and simmer for a further 30 minutes then add the milk and blend (blitz) thoroughly. Add more stock if required.

Potato and mint pea soup

Serves 4

What you will need:

1 litre of vegetable stock
4 large potatoes
1 onion
3 cups of frozen peas
Knob of butter
2 tablespoons of cream

What you will need to do:

Peel and chop the onion and potatoes and fry off with the butter for 5 minutes
Add to the stock and bring to a simmer
Simmer for 20 minutes and then blend (blitz) thoroughly
Serve with a swirl of cream

t and ginger soup

What you will need:

1 litre of vegetable stock
6 carrots
1 onion
2 tablespoons of grated ginger
2 tablespoons of cream
Half a teaspoon of cayenne pepper
Knob of butter

What you will need to do:

Peel and chop the carrots and the onion and fry off for a couple of minutes with the butter then add the grated ginger and the cayenne pepper and fry for another minute.
Add to the stock and bring to a simmer then simmer for 15 minutes and then add the cream blend (blitz) thoroughly with the cream

Cullen Skink

Serves 4-6

What you will need

(There is no need to use fish stock with this recipe)

2 large pieces of smoked haddock (undyed)
1 onion
2 knobs of butter
2 cups of milk
1 cup of cream
4 potatoes
1 bay leaf
Half a cup of parsley

What you will need to do

Put the haddock in a large pan and cover with the milk (add more milk if needed to just cover the fish. Add the bay leaf and bring to a gentle simmer and then simmer for 10 minutes

Peel and chop the onion and fry until soft in the butter

Remove the fish from the pan and put to the side until later

Peel and cube the potatoes and add to the milk liquor then simmer until potatoes are cooked then remove the bay leaf, add the cream and onions. Chop the parsley and add. Simmer for a further minute

Shellfish Soup

Serves 4-6

What you will need:

1 litre of rich shellfish stock
100g Clams
100g Cockles
100g Mussels
4 Razor fish
100g King prawns
1 cup of milk
Knob of butter
Half a cup of oatmeal

What you will need to do:

Put all the shellfish, except the prawns, in a pot, cover with water and bring to the boil. Simmer until cooked and remove any where the shells have remained closed.
Shell and de-vein the king prawns.
Remove all the shellfish and remove from the shells. Cut up the razor fish and then add the clams, mussels and razor fish to your prepared stock.
 Bring back to a gentle simmer, add the half cup of oatmeal, the knob of butter and the cup of milk. After five minutes add the de-shelled and de-veined

prawns. Switch off the heat, cover and let stand until the prawns cook in the residual heat.

Partan Bree (Crab Soup)

Serves 4-6

What you will need

Half a litre of shellfish stock
1 large crab
A quarter of a cup of rice
Two and a half cups of milk
Three quarters of a cup of cream
One tablespoon of chives

What you will need to do

Cook the crab and remove the meat, separating the brown and white meat
Cook the rice in the stock and the milk, add the brown meat and blend (blitz)
Add the white meat and mix through the cream
Garnish with chopped chives

Stews

Vegetable Hotch Potch
Serves 6-8

What you will need:

1 litres of vegetable stock
6 carrots
6 small white turnips
1 cup (128g) of dried peas
1 cup (128g) of broad beans
Small cauliflower
1 little gem lettuce
6 spring onions
Half a cup (65g) of curly leaf parsley

What you need to do:

Skin **half** of the peas and all of the broad beans and then   put half of the peas to one side
Bring stock to the boil and add the skinned peas and broad beans
Peel, cut and dice the carrots and the turnips and add to the pot then simmer for 40 minutes
Meantime cut the cauliflower into florets and chop the lettuce.
Cut the spring onions into small pieces. Chop the curly leaf parsley. After the initial 40 minutes simmer, add the remaining half cup of peas, the

cauliflower, lettuce and spring onions to the pot. Stir and then add the chopped parsley. This is a thick soup, but you can add more stock if you prefer it a little thinner.

Spicy Green Vegetable Stew

Serves 6-8

What you will need:

1 litre of vegetable stock
200 grams of green beans
200 grams of broad beans
Half a cup of frozen green peas
200 grams of broccoli
2 stalks of celery

Half a teaspoon of smoked paprika
Half a teaspoon of cumin
Half a teaspoon of chopped ginger
A quarter of a teaspoon of chili powder
Half a cup of green lentils
Knob of butter

What you need to do:

De-shell the broad beans. Remove the fibrous, stringy bits from the celery and finely chop. Wash and chop the green beans and wash and cut the broccoli into florets
Fry off the celery with the butter

Add the broad beans, green beans, peas and lentils to the stock and bring to a gentle simmer and add the celery and the spices. Simmer for 30 minutes

White Bean Stew

Serves 6-8

What you will need:

1 litre of vegetable stock
400g of haricot beans
400g of chickpeas
1 onion
2 sticks of celery
2 carrots
Half a cup of parsley
2 cloves of garlic
Knob of butter

What you need to do:

Chop the onions. Remove the fibrous, stringy bits from the celery. Finely dice the carrots and chop the garlic. Fry the onions, garlic and the celery in the butter until soft.

Add the haricot beans and chickpeas to the stock and bring to a gentle simmer then add the onions, garlic and celery.

Chop the parsley and add to the pot and simmer for a further minute.

Spicy Cauliflower and Potato Stew

Serves 6-8

What you will need:

1 litre of vegetable stock
1 large cauliflower
3 large potatoes
1 onion
2 stalks of celery

Half a teaspoon of smoked paprika
Half a teaspoon of cumin
Half a teaspoon of chopped ginger
A quarter of a teaspoon of chili powder
1 cup of cream
Knob of butter

What you need to do:

Dice the onion. Remove the fibrous, stringy bits from the celery and chop. Peel and dice the potatoes and cut the cauliflower into florets.
Fry off the onion and celery in the butter for a couple of minutes and add to the stock in a pot then add the potatoes, cauliflower and spices. Gently simmer for 20 minutes and then stir in the cream and simmer for a further minute

Barley and Root Vegetable Stew

Serves 6-8

What you will need:

1.5 litres of vegetable stock
3 large potatoes
Half a swede
3 large carrots
1 parsnip
1 cup of pearl barley
Half a cup of parsley

What you need to do:

Pre-soak the barley overnight in cold water, rinse and add to the stock. Bring to a simmer and simmer for 15 minutes.
Peel and dice the potatoes, carrots, swede and parsnip and add to the pot. Simmer for a further 20 minutes
Finely chop the parsley and add to the post before serving

Chili Bean and Tomato Stew

Serves 4-6

What you will need:

Half a litre of vegetable stock
4 large tomatoes
1 tin of chickpeas
1 tin of kidney beans
1 onion
One teaspoon of chilli powder (or to preference)
Half a teaspoon of celery salt
Half a teaspoon of garlic salt
Teaspoon of vegetable oil

What you need to do:

Blanche and skin the tomatoes and quarter
Chop the onion and fry off in vegetable oil with the chilli
Add the tomatoes, chickpeas, kidney beans and onions to the stock and simmer for 10 minutes

Mixed Lentil and Root Vegetable Stew

Serves 6-8

What you will need:

1.5 litres of vegetable stock
Half a cup of red lentils
A third of a cup of pay lentils
3 potatoes
Half of a swede
2 large carrots
1 parsnip

What you need to do:

Rinse and add the lentils to half of the stock and bring to a rolling simmer. Simmer for 10 minutes, stirring a few times.
Peel and cut into chunks the potatoes, swede and parsnip
Add the remaining stock to the pot alongside the vegetables, stir and simmer for a further 20 minutes

Curries

Mixed Vegetable Curry

<u>What you will need:</u>

1 teaspoon of coconut oil
1 potato
1 sweet potato
1 onion
1 carrot
Half a cauliflower
A handful of fine green beans
15oz can of chickpeas
2 tomatoes
2 cloves of garlic
Juice of 1 lime
1 cup of vegetable juice
1/2 cup of frozen garden peas
1 teaspoon of chili powder
1 teaspoon of fenugreek
1 teaspoon of cumin
1 teaspoon of turmeric
1 teaspoon of Nigella seeds
1 teaspoon of coriander
1 teaspoon of onion salt
Salt and pepper to taste

What you will need to do:

Peel and chop the onion, carrot and potatoes. Cut cauliflower into florets. Trim the green beans. Mince the garlic. Cut the tomatoes into quarters

To the oil in the pan, add the chopped onions and all of the spices. Gently brown, then add the garlic. Fry for a minute and then add the potato, the cauliflower and the carrot. Mix and coat thoroughly then add the sweet potato, the coconut milk and the vegetable stock. Bring to a gentle simmer and simmer for 10 minutes then add the chickpeas and simmer for a further 10 minutes before adding the green beans, the tomatoes and the frozen peas. Simmer for a further 10 minutes then add the lime juice and season to taste.

Carrot and Coriander Curry

<u>What you will need:</u>

2 tablespoons of butter
2 onions
2 cloves of garlic
2 large carrots
1 teaspoon of ground cumin
¼ teaspoon of smoked paprika
¼ teaspoon of ground chili
1 teaspoon of curry powder
2 cups of vegetable stock
3 tablespoons of chopped coriander
2 tablespoons of cream

<u>What you will need to do:</u>

Peel and chop the onions
Peel and dice the carrots
Mince the garlic
Melt the butter in a pan and fry the onions, garlic and carrots until soft
Mix through the cumin, smoked paprika, chili and curry powder and cook off for another minute, then add the vegetable stock
Simmer gently until it reduces by half
Add the chopped coriander and the cream, stir and serve

Potato and Chickpea Curry

What you will need:

2 tablespoons extra virgin olive oil
1 onion
4 cloves of garlic
4 teaspoons curry powder
1 ½ teaspoons paprika
1 teaspoon cayenne pepper
2 teaspoons cumin powder
½ teaspoon allspice
2 teaspoons fresh ginger
½ teaspoon black pepper
4 large potatoes
15 oz can of chickpeas
1 cup vegetable stock
1 tablespoon lemon juice
14 oz can of chopped tomatoes
14 oz can of coconut milk
salt

What you will need to do:

Peel and dice the onion and the potatoes
Mince the garlic
Heat the oil in a large pan and a dd the onion and fry gently for about 3 minutes, until translucent then add the garlic and fry for about 2 minutes

Add the curry powder, paprika, cayenne, cumin, allspice, ginger, salt, and pepper. Stir and cook for about 2 minutes until the spices are fragrant.

Add the potatoes and mix well until well-coated in spices. Then add the chickpeas and stir to incorporate.

Add the vegetable stock, lemon juice, and tomatoes and stir, then pour in the coconut milk and stir to combine.

Simmer on a medium heat and cook for 15-20 minutes, until the potatoes are tender and easily pierced with a fork.

Sweet Potato Curry

<u>What you will need:</u>

1 tbsp coconut oil
1 onion
2 garlic cloves
1 tablespoon of grated ginger
¼ teaspoon chili powder
¼ teaspoon smoked paprika
½ teaspoon cumin
2 tomatoes
1 tablespoon of smooth peanut butter
5 large sweet potatoes
14oz can of coconut milk
1 cup of vegetable stock
Two handfuls of spinach
Juice of 1 lime
Salt and pepper to taste

<u>What you will need to do:</u>

Peel and chop the onion and grate the garlic
Peel and cube the potatoes
Blanche, peel and de-seed the tomatoes and then chop
In a saucepan, soften the onions in the coconut oil and then add the garlic and the ginger. Cook for a

minute and then add the spices, the peanut butter and the cubed potatoes

Mix thoroughly and then add the coconut milk and vegetable stock

Bring to a gentle simmer and simmer until potatoes are soft, be careful not to over stir and break up the potatoes

Mix through the spinach, add the lime juice and season to taste with salt and pepper

Kidney Bean Curry

What you will need:

1 tablespoon of vegetable oil
1 onion
2 cloves of garlic
2 teaspoons of grated ginger
2 handfuls coriander
1 teaspoon of cumin
1 teaspoon of smoked paprika
2 teaspoons of garam masala
1 14oz can of chopped tomatoes
1 14oz can of kidney beans (n water)
Salt and pepper to taste

What you will need to do:

Peel and chop the onion and mince the garlic
Chop the coriander leaves roughly and cut the stalks finely
In a frying pan, add the chopped onion to the oil and fry until soft then add the garlic, ginger and the coriander stalks
Cook for a couple of minutes then add the cumin, paprika and garam masala and mix thoroughly. Cook for another minute and add the can of chopped tomatoes and kidney beans with their water

Bring to a gentle simmer and then simmer for 15 minutes
Season with the salt and pepper and add the coriander leaves

Cauliflower Curry

What you will need:

1 whole cauliflower
1 teaspoon of coriander
1 teaspoon of cumin
1 teaspoon of fenugreek
1 teaspoon of chili powder
1 teaspoon of ginger
2 red onions
2 green chilies
4 cloves of garlic
14oz can of coconut milk
2 large tomatoes
Juice of 1 lime
1 tablespoon of coconut oil
½ teaspoon of salt

What you will need to do:

Peel and chop the red onions and add to a wok with the coconut oil. Fry until beginning to soften
Cut the cauliflower into florets and chop the tomatoes
Mince the garlic and add to the onions then add the fenugreek, cumin, coriander, chili powder and ginger. Fry for a minute

Add the cauliflower florets and completely coat with the ingredients and stir-fry for 5 minutes then add the can of tomatoes and stir-fry for another 5 minutes
De-seed and finely chop the green chillies and add to the pan. Fry for another minute
Add the coconut milk and the salt and bring to a gentle simmer. Simmer until cauliflower is tender and then add the lime juice.

Pasta Dishes

Roasted Red Pepper Spaghetti

What you will need:

2 red bell peppers
2 tablespoons of extra virgin olive oil
2 medium shallot
4 cloves garlic
Sea salt and ground black pepper (to taste)
1 ½ cups of unsweetened almond milk
1 Tablespoon of nutritional yeast
1 ½ tablespoons of corn flour
200g of spaghetti
2 tablespoons of grated parmesan
Handful of basil leaves

What you will need to do:

Roast the red peppers on a baking sheet in a hot oven then cover in foil for 10 minutes before peeling off the skin. Remove the stalks and seed
Cook the spaghetti in salted boiling water until al dente
Peel and finely chop the shallots and finely chop the garlic and fry gently in the olive oil until soft then season with salt and pepper to taste

Add the onion and garlic to a food processor along with the peppers and the almond milk, the nutritional yeast and the corn flour and blend until creamy. Add more seasoning if required

Put the mixture in a pan and simmer gently to thicken and then add the spaghetti and mix thoroughly

Top with parmesan and basil

Spaghetti with cabbage

<u>What you will need:</u>

2 large handfuls fresh chunky breadcrumbs
3 tablespoons of olive oil
3 garlic cloves,
200g penne pasta
1 onion
½ a cup of white wine
Zest of ½ a lemon
2 Tablespoons of crème fraiche
½ small head Savoy cabbage

<u>What you will need to do:</u>

<u>Finely chop the garlic</u>
<u>Finely slice the cabbage</u>
In a bowl, mix the breadcrumbs with half the oil and 1 garlic clove, and season well. Spread out on a large baking tray and bake for 8 minutes in a moderate to high oven until crisp and golden. Remove and set aside.

Cook the pasta in a large pan of boiling water until al dente. Meanwhile, pour the remaining oil into a frying pan, add the onion and remaining garlic, season and cook for about 4 minutes until golden, then add the wine and lemon zest. Reduce for a few minutes, then add the crème fraiche. Remove from heat but keep warm.

Add the cabbage to the pasta water for the last 3 minutes of cooking time. Drain and return to the pan, add the creamy sauce to the pasta and toss together. Divide between 2 bowls and top with the crumbs.

Spaghetti and Sardines

What you will need:

400g spaghetti
1 tablespoon of olive oil
2 garlic cloves, crushed
A pinch of chili flakes
can of chopped tomato
2 cans skinless and boneless sardines in tomato sauce
Handful of pitted black olives
1 tablespoon of capers
small handful of parsley

What you will need to do:

Crush the garlic cloves and chop the olives and the parsley
Cook the spaghetti in a large pan of boiling salted water until al dente.
Heat the oil in a medium pan and cook the garlic for 1 minute. Add the chilli flakes, tomatoes and sardines, breaking up roughly with a wooden spoon. Heat for 2-3 minutes, then stir in the olives, capers and most of the parsley. Mix well to combine.
Drain the pasta, reserving a couple of tablespoons of the water. Add the pasta to the sauce and mix well, adding the reserved water if the sauce is a little thick.

Divide between 4 bowls and sprinkle with the remaining parsley.

Spicy Spaghetti with Garlic Mushrooms

What you will need:

250g pack chestnut mushroom, thickly sliced
1 garlic clove
small bunch of parsley leaves
1 stalk of celery
stick, finely chopped
1 onion
A can of chopped tomatoes
½ a teaspoon of dried chili flakes
300g spaghetti

What you will need to do:

Dice the onion. Slice the mushrooms and the garlic and de-vein and finely chop the parsley.
Heat 1 tablespoon of the oil in a pan, then add the mushrooms, and fry over a high heat for 3minutess until golden and softened.
Add the garlic, fry for 1 minute more, then tip into a bowl with the parsley. Add the onion and celery to the pan with the rest of the oil, then fry for 5 minutes until lightly coloured.
Stir in the tomatoes, chilli and a little salt, then bring to the boil. Reduce the heat and simmer, uncovered,

for 10 minutes until thickened.

Boil the spaghetti in salted water, then drain. Toss with the sauce and top with the garlicky mushrooms.

Lentil Spaghetti Bolognaise

<u>What you will need:</u>

400g of spaghetti
1 cup of red lentils
1 onion
2 cloves of garlic
Teaspoon of mixed Italian herbs
1 stick of celery
4 mushrooms
4 tomatoes
1 tablespoon of tomato paste
1 cup of vegetable stock
1 tablespoon of extra virgin olive oil
Salt and pepper to taste

<u>What you will need to do:</u>

Peel and chop the onions and add to the olive oil in a pan, fry gently until soft
Mince the garlic, chop the tomatoes, peel and chop the carrots,
de-vein and chop the celery
chop the mushrooms
add the mushrooms to the pan and fry for 3 or 4 minutes until mushrooms are cooked

Add the vegetable stock, the garlic, tomato paste, celery, carrots and the lentils and bring to a rolling simmer, cover and reduce the heat

Cook for approximately 20 minutes and add more stock if required

Cook the spaghetti in salted water until al dente

Add the cooked spaghetti to the sauce and mix through

Asparagus Carbonara

What you will need:

400g penne pasta
2 eggs
1 bunch of asparagus
5 cloves of garlic
1/2 cup of white wine
1 cup of grated cheddar cheese
2 tablespoons of extra virgin olive oil
1 tablespoon of fresh parsley
Salt and pepper to taste

What you will need to do:
Chop the garlic finely
Slice and toss the asparagus in a little olive oil, season with salt and put in a pre-heated medium oven. After 5 minutes mix through the chopped garlic and keep in the oven for another 5 minutes
Reduce the wine in a small pan by half then take off the heat
Cook the pasta in salted water until al dente
Whisk the eggs with the remaining olive oil and add the cooked pasta. Mix thoroughly and add the wine and the cheese
Add the asparagus
Serve with a sprinkling of chopped parsley

Mac and Cheese (1) Broccoli and salmon

What you will need:

250g penne
1 head of broccoli
1 tablespoon of butter
25g plain flour
2 cups of milk
100g mascarpone
8 sundried tomatoes
2 tablespoons of small capers
8 anchovies
fillets, halved (optional)
2 handfuls of fresh basil leaves
4 fresh skinless salmon fillets
1 cup of grated mature cheddar cheese
Salt and pepper to taste

What you will need to do:

Cut the broccoli into florets and thinly slice the sundried tomatoes. Half the anchovies and roughly tear the basil leaves
Cook the penne in boiling salted water for about six minute and then add the broccoli and boil until the broccoli is just tender then drain.

Whilst the pasta is cooking, put the butter, flour and milk in a large pan and heat, stirring continuously, until it thickens to make a smooth sauce. Remove from the heat and stir in the mascarpone, sun-dried tomatoes, capers, anchovies and basil, then add the pasta and broccoli and season well with salt and pepper

Halve the salmon fillets width ways, then place the pieces in a single layer on the base of an ovenproof dish. Spoon the broccoli mixture on top, then scatter with the grated cheddar and bake in a moderate oven for 30 minutes.

Mac and Cheese (2) onion

What you will need:

5 tablespoons of butter
2 onions
225g of spiral pasta
2 tablespoons of plain flour
2 cups of milk
2 cups of grated cheddar cheese
1 cup of grated Gruyere cheese
1 teaspoon of Dijon mustard
Pinch of cayenne pepper
1 teaspoon of fresh thyme leaves, plus more for garnish
Salt and pepper to taste

What you will need to do:

Thinly slice the onions
Brush 4 to 6 ramekins (depending on size) with butter
In a large pan, melt 3 tablespoons of the butter over a medium heat, then add the onions and a pinch of salt and cook, stirring occasionally, until they are golden, about 30 minutes.
Cook pasta in a large pot of boiling salted water until al dente then drain

In a medium saucepan, melt the remaining 2 tablespoons butter over medium-high.

Add flour and cook, stirring, 1 minute. While whisking, slowly pour in milk until combined. Bring to a boil and reduce heat to medium.

Simmer, stirring, until sauce is thickened, about 6 minutes then stir in the cheddar cheese and half of the gruyere, and when the cheese has melted remove from the heat and add the pasta to the sauce.

Stir in the caramelised onions, Dijon, thyme, and cayenne. Season with salt and pepper.

Divide the mixture amongst the ramekins and top each ramekin with the remaining gruyere.

Bake until sauce is bubbly around the edges, about 20 minutes.

Switch oven to grill and grill until cheese is golden, about 2 minutes. Garnish with more thyme before serving.

Mac and Cheese (3)
Butternut squash, leek and pea

What you will need:

1 small butternut squash
2 small leeks
400 g macaroni
2 tomatoes
2 tablespoons of butter
40 g plain flour
2 cups of milk
1 tablespoon of wholegrain mustard
Juice of half a lemon
1 cup of grated cheddar cheese
1 cup of fresh breadcrumbs
1 tablespoon of olive oil

What you will need to do:

Peel and slice the squash into medium sized cubes
Wash and slice the leeks and slice the tomatoes
Place the cubes of squash on an oven tray, drizzle over the olive oil and cook in a moderate to high oven until cooked through.
Cook the macaroni in salted boiling water until al dente.
Melt the butter, and then add leeks and cook until soft then stir in the flour and the milk and bring to

the boil, stirring all the time to avoid lumps. Add mustard and lemon juice to taste

Place the macaroni, squash and sauce in an oven-proof dish and top with the breadcrumbs, grated cheese and tomato slices.

Bake in the oven for about 25 minutes till nicely browned on top.

Mac and Cheese (4) Tuna

What you will need:

250g macaroni
2 tablespoons of butter
1/4 cup of plain flour
1 garlic clove
2 1/2 cups of milk
A 425g can of flaked tuna in spring water
1 cup frozen garden peas
1 1/2 cups grated cheddar cheese
Salt and pepper to taste

What you will need to do:

Crush the garlic and drain the tuna. Preheat grill on high. Grease a 5cm deep, 18cm square (base), baking dish. Cook macaroni in a saucepan of boiling, salted water, until al dente. Drain. Return to pan.

Melt butter in a saucepan over a medium heat. Add the flour and the crushed garlic and stir until the mixture thickens and bubbles then remove from heat.

Gradually whisk in milk. Return to heat. Cook, stirring, for 5 minutes or until thickened. Remove from heat.

Add the tuna, peas and 1 cup of the cheese. Stir until the cheese melts then stir in pasta. Spoon mixture into an oven-proof dish. Sprinkle with remaining cheese. Grill for 4 to 5 minutes or until cheese browns and melts.

Lasagna Crab Rolls

What you will need:

2 large eggs
2 cups of cottage cheese
1/4 cup grated Parmesan cheese
2 tablespoons Italian seasoning
2 tablespoons finely chopped fresh parsley
1 teaspoon dried oregano
1/2 teaspoon dried basil
1/2 teaspoon dried thyme
1/4 teaspoon garlic powder
2 small cans of prepared crab meat
12 lasagne sheets
3 cups of the spicy tomato catsup (see the recipe under Catsups)
Salt and pepper to taste

What you will need to do:

Beat the eggs. Cook the lasagna sheets in boiling salted water and drain.
In a large bowl, combine the eggs, cheeses and the herbs. Season with salt and pepper to taste, then add crab and mix well.
Share the mixture between each sheet of lasagna and roll up.

Place seam side down in a 13x9-in. baking dish coated with cooking spray. Top with tomato sauce. Cover and bake in a moderate oven for 30-40 minutes.

Lasagna Pesto Rolls

What you will need:

1 1/2 cups ricotta cheese
3/4 cup pesto sauce
8 lasagne sheets, cooked and drained
3 1/2 cups of spicy tomato catsup
1 cup shredded mozzarella cheese
1/4 cup grated Parmesan cheese

What you will need to do:

Cook the lasagne sheets in boiling salted water and drain

In a medium bowl, stir together the ricotta cheese with 1/2 a cup of the prepared pesto.

Divide the mixture between the 8 lasagne sheets, ensuring that you spread the mixture the length of each sheet.

Divide 1 cup of the tomato catsup among the 8 lasagne sheets, spreading it atop the ricotta mixture.

Add 1 1/2 cups of the remaining tomato catsup to the bottom of a 13x9-inch baking dish.

Roll up the lasagne sheets then arrange them seam side down in the baking dish. Top them with the remaining 1 cup of tomato catsup and 1/4 cup of the prepared pesto. Cover the baking dish securely with foil then bake it for 30 minutes.

Remove the foil, top the roll-ups with the mozzarella cheese and continue baking, uncovered, an additional 5 minutes or until the cheese is melted.

Remove the dish from the oven, top the lasagne rolls with the grated Parmesan cheese and serve.

Lasagna with Roast Vegetables

What you will need:

3 red peppers
2 aubergines
8 tablespoons of olive oil
3 cups of roasted tomato sauce (see recipe in savoury sauces)
12 lasagna sheets
3 cups of white sauce (see recipe)
125g ball mozzarella
8 cherry tomatoes
3 cloves of garlic
1 teaspoon of onion powder
Salt and pepper to taste

What you will need to do:

Core and de-seed the peppers and cut into chunks. Halve the tomatoes. Trim the ends off the aubergines and slice. Place onto a baking tray and rub in the olive oil. Throw in the 3 whole garlic cloves.
Roast in a moderate oven, mixing a couple of times, until soft then remove the garlic cloves, squeeze out of their skins and mix through the vegetables.
Put a layer of the vegetables in a greased oven-proof dish, top with a third of the tomato sauce ad hen layer with lasagne sheets. Top the lasagne sheets with a

third of the white sauce and repeat until you have 3 layers of pasta and finish with the final third of the white sauce.

Scatter the mozzarella cheese on top and bake in a moderate oven until bubbling and golden 9about 40 minutes.

Lasagna with Courgettes and Mushrooms

What you will need:

3 cups of roasted tomato sauce (see recipe)
4 medium courgettes
6 whole milk mozzarella balls
1/4 cup parmesan cheese
8 chestnut mushrooms
Handful of shiitake mushrooms
1 onion
1 tablespoon olive oil
4 cloves of garlic
1 teaspoon of dried oregano
1 teaspoon of dried thyme
1 teaspoon of red pepper flakes
Salt and pepper to taste
1 tablespoon fresh basil chopped for garnish

What you will need to do:

Shred the mozzarella. Dice the mushrooms and the onion. Slice the garlic.
Thinly slice the courgettes lengthwise and season with salt. After 10 minutes dry off the slices by blotting with kitchen paper then put a single on a lined baking sheet and bake for 10 minutes.

Heat the oil in a pan and add the red pepper flakes and the garlic and stir and fry off for 30 seconds. Add the onion, season with salt and pepper and fry until onions are soft then add the mushrooms, oregano and thyme.

Fry until mushrooms are browned.

Layer the courgetti in the bottom of a greased oven-proof dish and alternately build the layers with the tomato sauce, the mushroom mixture and a sprinkling of parmesan.

Finish off by covering the final layer with the mozzarella. Bake in a moderate oven until the cheese is bubbling and browned and garnish with the chopped basil leaves.

Creamy Courgette Pasta

What you will need:

4 courgettes
1 clove of garlic
Handful of grated parmesan cheese
Small tub of crème fraiche
300g of tagliatelle
Teaspoon of extra virgin olive oil
Black pepper

What you will need to do:
Grate the courgettes
Mince the garlic
To a pan, add the oil, heat and then add the minced garlic fry gently for a few seconds and then add the grated courgettes. Mix thoroughly and fry for 2 or 3 minutes
Meantime cook the tagliatelle in salted boiling water until al dente. When drained, keep a cup of the water and add to the courgette mix along with the crème fraiche and the tagliatelle. Mix thoroughly and add the parmesan.
Season with black pepper

Dishes with Pulses and Beans

Lentil Loaf

What you will need:

1 cup of red lentils
2 cups of vegetable stock
1 tablespoon of extra virgin olive oil
1 onion
2 cloves of garlic
1 spring onion
1 carrot
½ a red bell pepper
½ a green bell pepper
1 egg
Salt and pepper to taste

What you will need to do:

Cook the lentils in the vegetable stock for about 20 minutes
Chop the onion, the spring onion, the peppers, and the garlic and add to a frying pan with the olive oil. Fry until the vegetables are tender
Grate the carrot
Beat the egg
Mix all the cooked vegetables in a bowl with the egg, and the grated carrot, add the lentils and season with salt and pepper

Pour the mixture into a lined and greased 500g loaf tin and bake in a medium oven for 20 minutes
Allow to stand for 5 minutes and then turn out

Lentil Burgers

<u>What you will need:</u>

1 cup puy lentils
2 cups of vegetable stock
2 garlic cloves
6 chestnut mushrooms
¼ teaspoon of smoked paprika
4 tablespoons of extra-virgin olive oil
¼ cup of flour

<u>What you will need to do:</u>

Grate the garlic and finely chop the mushrooms.
Cook the lentils in the vegetable stock for about 10 minutes until tender. Drain very well in a fine-mesh sieve, then let cool.
Add the paprika with 2 Tablespoons of the olive oil, and remaining garlic clove with the mushrooms and mix thoroughly.
Add the lentils to the mushroom mix and stir and mash them with the back of a spoon or a potato masher until lentils are partly mashed but with lots of whole lentils still remaining. Vigorously stir in flour until mixture holds together when squeezed; if it doesn't, continue to mash until it does and add 1–2

tablespoons of flour if needed. Form into 6 patties about ¾" thick.

Fry in olive oil until deeply browned.

Working in 2 batches, heat 1 Tbsp. oil in a large nonstick

Lentil and Black Bean Chili

<u>What you will need:</u>

3 tablespoons olive oil
1 large red onion
2 stalks celery
4 medium to large carrots
4 cloves garlic
4 tablespoons chili powder
1 tablespoons paprika
1 teaspoon allspice
1/2 teaspoon cumin
1 bay leaf
5 - 6 cups vegetable stock
2 cups of red lentils
3 cups of roasted tomato sauce (see recipe)
29 ounce can black beans drained and rinsed
1 cup frozen sweet corn
12 ounce jar roasted red peppers diced
1 - 2 teaspoons Tabasco sauce
salt and pepper to taste

<u>What you will need to do:</u>

Dice the onion, celery and carrots and mince the garlic

In a large heavy pot over medium high heat, add the olive oil, then the onion, celery and carrots. Sauté until the onions have softened, then add the garlic and continue to cook for just one minute.

Add the spices and the bay leaf. Cook for about two more minutes to get them fragrant.

Add the vegetable stock, the lentils and the tomato sauce and raise the heat to high, bringing the mixture to a gentle simmer and simmer for about 30 minutes to get the lentils tender.

Add the black beans, corn, red peppers and Tabasco and continue to cook for about 20 more minutes. Add additional vegetable stock if required.

Puy Lentils with Broccoli

What you will need:

1 large head of broccoli
2 teaspoons of smoked paprika
1 cup of puy lentils
1 clove of garlic
Zest of ½ a lemon
Juice of 1 lemon
½ cup of Greek yoghurt
1 tablespoon of chopped parsley
2 tablespoons of chopped almonds
Salt and pepper to taste

What you will need to do:

Rinse and cook the lentils in slightly salted boiling water for about 20 minutes until cooked through
Cut the broccoli into 4 pieces and place on a baking tray with the stalk side down
Mix the olive oil, the paprika and salt and pepper in a bowl and then rub over the broccoli
Place the broccoli in a preheated medium oven for 30 minutes and then pour over the cooked lentils
Mix the minced garlic, lemon zest and juice with the yogurt. Season to taste and add a splash of water. Remove the broccoli from the oven, sprinkle over the

parsley and serve topped with the yoghurt mix and a sprinkle of chopped almonds

Puy Lentil Hotpot

<u>What you will need:</u>

1 cup of puy lentils
1 onion
1 sweet potato
1 potato
8 Portobello mushrooms
2 cloves of garlic
2 tablespoons of olive oil
1 ½ teaspoons of ground cumin
1 teaspoon of smoked paprika
1 tablespoon of soy sauce
1 tablespoon of balsamic vinegar
1 teaspoon of thyme

<u>What you will need to do:</u>

Cook the lentils in slightly boiling water for about 20 minutes until cooked
Peel and slice the potatoes and cook in slightly boiling water for about 3 minutes. Drain
Chop the onion and fry until soft with half the olive oil
Slice and add the mushrooms. Fry for 3 or 4 minutes then mince and add the garlic

Mix through and add the cumin and the paprika and cook for another minute then add the lentils, the soy sauce, and the vinegar

Season to taste and pour into a casserole dish

Layer the part-cooked potatoes over the mixture in the casserole dish and brush over the remaining olive oil

Place in a pre-heated medium oven and cook for about 20 minutes until potatoes are crisp

Remove from the oven and sprinkle over the thyme

Aubergine and Lentil Bake

What you will need:

2 aubergines
1 cup pf puy lentils
2 onions
2 cloves of garlic
Half a butternut squash
1 can of chopped tomatoes
4 tablespoons of extra virgin olive oil
½ a cup of vegetable stock
1 ball of mozzarella cheese
Salt and pepper to taste

What you will need to do:

Cook the lentils for 20 minutes in slightly boiling water
Slice the aubergines and rub in 2 tablespoons of the olive oil. Place of a baking tray and put in a pre-heated medium oven and bake for 20 minutes
Chop the onions and mince the garlic and add to a frying pan with the remaining olive oil. Fry until the onions are soft
Cube the squash and add to the frying pan with the can of chopped tomatoes and the vegetable stock

Bring to a gentle simmer and simmer for 15 minutes and then add the cooked lentils

Season to taste with the salt and pepper

In a small baking dish, alternatively layer the lentil mix and the sliced aubergine, ensuring the top layer is aubergine

Break up the cheese over the top, return to the oven and bake for a further 10 to 15 minutes

Lentil Casserole with Roasted Root Vegetables

What you will need:

1 onion
2 cloves of garlic
2 large potatoes
4 carrots
2 parsnips
Half a butternut squash
Half a small swede
1 pint of vegetable stock
1 cup of red lentils
2 tablespoons of extra virgin olive oil
¼ teaspoon of chili powder
½ teaspoon of ground cumin
½ teaspoon of turmeric
½ teaspoon of smoked paprika
2 tablespoons of chopped coriander

What you will need to do:

Peel and chop all of the vegetables. Crush the garlic. Mix thoroughly with the olive oil and place on a baking tray. Roast in a pre-heated medium to hot oven for 30 minutes, stirring occasionally.
Cook the lentils in the vegetable stock

Remove the vegetables from the oven and place in a casserole dish

Stir in the spices and add the cooked lentils with any stock remaining

Mix in half of the coriander

Return to the oven and continue baking for a further 10 minutes

Serve sprinkled with the remaining coriander

Black Bean Meatless Balls

What you will need:

15oz. can of Black Beans
1 cup of oat flour
2 cups of rolled oats
Half a cup of fresh breadcrumbs
1 tablespoon of vegetable oil
1 teaspoon of smoked paprika
1 teaspoon of garlic powder
1 teaspoon of onion powder
Salt and pepper to taste

What you will need to do:

Drain the black beans and rinse till water runs clear, fill the can back up with water and pour it and the beans into a food processor, and pulse till smooth. Combine the flour, the rolled oats and the bean purée and mix through the paprika, garlic and onion powder. Season with salt and pepper then rest for 5 minutes before dividing the mixture into equal sized balls, rolling each in the breadcrumbs and then frying in the oil until dark golden brown.

Courgette Noodles, white Beans and Tomatoes

What you will need:

200g spaghetti
2 medium courgettes
1/4 cup extra virgin olive oil
6 cloves of garlic
1 teaspoon of pinch of red pepper flakes
A can of cannellini beans, drained and rinsed
6 cherry tomatoes
Handful of fresh basil leaves
2 Tablespoons of Parmesan cheese

What you will need to do:

Use a spiral machine to make spirals from the courgettes.
Halve the tomatoes, slice the garlic and roughly tear the basil leaves.
Cook the spaghetti in salted boiling water until al dente and drain then mix through the courgetti noodles, allowing the heat from the spaghetti to begin to cook them
Add the garlic and the pepper flakes to a little olive oil in a pan and fry for a couple of minutes then add the beans, the tomatoes, and the courgette and

spaghetti mix to the pan and toss so that the noodles are fully coated. Gently warm through and cook until the courgetti noodles are soft then stir in the basil and garnish with the parmesan.

Butter Bean and Sweet Potato Hash

What you will need:

1 can of butterbeans
1 tablespoon olive oil
1 onion, finely diced
3 garlic cloves, finely chopped
1 large sweet potato, peeled and cut into 1.5 cm/1/2 inch cubes
2 carrots, diced
1 tablespoon freshly chopped rosemary leaves
3 freshly chopped sage leaves
2 cups vegetable stock
Sea salt and freshly ground black pepper, to taste
Roughly chopped fresh parsley, to garnish

What you will need to do:

Dice the onion and carrot, and finely chop the garlic. Peel the sweet potato and cut into chunky cubes.
In a large saucepan, heat the olive oil over a medium heat. Add the onion and cook, stirring occasionally, for about 5 minutes, until softened. Add the garlic and cook for 1 minute more. Stir in the sweet potato, carrots, rosemary and sage. Season well with salt and cook for another 2–3 minutes until the herbs are fragrant.

Add the drained butter beans and the vegetable stock and bring everything to a boil. Simmer over a medium-low heat, covered with a lid for 20 minutes until the sweet potato has softened.

Uncover, stir and simmer for a final 5 minutes. Crush the butter beans and chunks of potato against the side of the pot with a wooden spoon to release their starch and to thicken the hash. Season with salt and pepper to taste and garnish with the chopped parsley

Edamame and Chickpea Burgers

What you will need:

2 cups frozen edamame
1 can chickpeas, with liquid
2 cups of mushrooms
1/2 cup finely ground raw cashews
1/2 cup nutritional yeast
4 cloves garlic
1/2 teaspoon ground cumin
1 teaspoon of soy sauce
Salt and pepper, to taste
3 1/2 cups (420 g) chickpea flour
Oil, for frying

What you will need to do:

Shell the edamame beans then place them and the entire can of chickpeas, including the liquid, in a pan and warm through

Slice the mushrooms and mince the garlic

In a food processor, combine the edamame, chickpeas and liquid, mushrooms, cashews, yeast, garlic, cumin and soy sauce. Mix until smooth and then season with salt and pepper to taste

Transfer to a large bowl and slowly add and mix the chickpea flour until thick

Put in the fridge for 20 to 30 minutes to stiffen the mixture

Form into 16 patties.

Heat the oil in a frying pan and fry the patties for 4 to 5 minutes, or until golden brown on both sides

Savoury Rice Dishes

Spicy Tomato rice

What you will need:

1 cp of long grain rice
1 cup of vegetable stock
1 cup of passata
1 teaspoon of ground cumin
1 teaspoon of mild chilli powder
handful flat-leaf parsley

What you will need to do:

Place the rice in a pan with the stock and passata. Bring to the boil, cover and simmer for 10-12 minutes. Take off the heat, stir in the cumin and chili powder, then cover and rest for 5 minutes more. Fluff with a fork and serve scattered with parsley.

Egg fried rice

<u>What you will need:</u>

3 large eggs
2 tablespoons of peanut oil
1 red onion
1 carrot
1 red pepper
Half a cup of frozen peas
3 spring onions
1 cup of jasmine rice
2 cups of vegetable stock
2 1/2 tablespoons soy sauce
1/2 teaspoon five-spice powder
1 teaspoon of toasted sesame oil

<u>What you will need to do:</u>

Dice the onion and the carrot. Core and de-seed the pepper. Chop the spring onions and keep the white and green bits separate.
Cook the rice in the vegetable stock and allow to cool. Crack 3 eggs into a small bowl and beat them together.
Heat a wok (or large sauté pan) with 1/2 tablespoon of the oil over medium-high heat. Once the pan is hot, add the beaten eggs and scramble them for about a

minute. Transfer the eggs to a dish and turn off the heat. Wipe off the wok with a kitchen towel.

Drizzle the remaining 1 1/2 tablespoons of oil in the wok over medium-high heat.

Add the onions and cook them for about 2 minutes, stirring constantly.

Add the carrot and the pepper and white parts of the scallions and cook for another minute.

Add the cooked rice into the pan or wok and cook for a few minutes, until the rice is heated through.

Add the soy sauce, sesame oil, and five-spice powder and stir to distribute the seasonings.

Add the scrambled eggs and stir to mix again. Garnish with remaining sliced scallions.

Vegetable Fried Rice

<u>What you will need:</u>

½ small red onion
1 carrot
4 chestnut mushrooms
1 green bell pepper
¼ cup peas
1 spring onion
Handful of bean sprouts
3 cups cooked white rice
2 eggs
2 tablespoons oil
2 teaspoons of dark soy sauce
1 teaspoon of light soy sauce
1 teaspoon salt
Pinch of white pepper

<u>What you will need to do:</u>

Dice the onion and the carrot. Core and de-seed the pepper and dice. Finely chop the spring onion.
Cook the rice in the vegetable stock and leave to cool. Beat two eggs in a bowl and scramble them in a pan using one tablespoon of oil.
Cut the scrambled eggs with your spatula so you don't get large clumps of egg. Remove them from the pan and set aside.

Heat the wok on the highest setting and add 1 tablespoon of oil, red onion and carrots and stir for about 30 seconds.

Next, add the mushroom, peppers, and peas and stir-fry for another 30 seconds.

Add in your rice. Stir the mixture together for a minute to heat up the rice.

Add the bean sprouts, then add the dark soy sauce, salt, light soy sauce, and white pepper and stir-fry for another minute.

Add your egg and give it a final mix. Garnish with the spring onion.

Prawn and Egg Fried Rice

What you will need:

6 teaspoons of sunflower oil
3 eggs
2 small red chilies
6 spring onions
2 garlic cloves
400g peeled tiger prawns
200g white rice
1/3 cup soy sauce
1 teaspoon sesame oil
2 tablespoons sweet chili sauce
1 cup of frozen peas
Handful of coriander leaves

What you will need to do:

De-seed and finely chop the chilies
Finely shred the spring onions and the garlic
Lightly beat the eggs
Heat 2 teaspoons sunflower oil in a wok or large frying pan over medium- high heat. Add the egg and cook, stirring, for 1-2 minutes until softly scrambled. Remove egg from the pan and set aside.

Add remaining 4 teaspoons of sunflower oil to the pan, then add the chili, spring onion and garlic, stir through and fry for about one minute.

Add the prawns and cook for 2-3 minutes until opaque. Return egg to the pan with rice, soy, sesame oil, sweet chili sauce and peas, then cook, stirring, for 2-3 minutes to warm through.

Garnish with coriander

Mushroom Rice

<u>What you will need:</u>

3 tablespoons of extra virgin olive oil
2 tablespoons of butter
12 chestnut mushrooms
3 shitake mushrooms
2 garlic cloves
1 red onion
1 1/2 cups long grain rice
2 1/4 cups of vegetable stock
4 spring onions
Salt and pepper to taste

<u>What you will need to do</u>:

Chop the mushrooms, dice the red onion and finely chop the garlic

Heat 2 tablespoons oil in a large pot over high heat. Add half the mushrooms, and cook for 5 minutes until golden. Season with salt and pepper then remove and set aside

Add the remaining tablespoon of oil and add the butter to the pan. When the butter is melted, add onions and garlic.

Cook for 30 seconds, then add remaining mushrooms. Cook for 5 minutes or until mushrooms are lightly browned.

Add rice and a splash of vegetable stock and mix, then add the remaining stock.

Cover bring to a simmer then turn down to medium low.

Cook for 15 minutes or until there is no residual liquid

Remove from stove, remove lid and mix in the spring onions then recover and leave for 10 minutes before serving

Spicy Mixed Pepper Rice

<u>What you will need:</u>

4 Cups Cooked Rice
1 red bell pepper
1 green bell pepper
1 yellow or orange bell pepper
2 red onions
4 Garlic Cloves
2 teaspoons of sweet chilli sauce
2 spring onions
1 tbsp Oil

What you will need to do:

Core and de-seed the peppers and then dice. Dice the red onions. Finely chop the garlic and the spring onions.

In a pan heat the oil and add finely chopped garlic. Sauté for a 1-2 minutes, and then add the red onions and sauté until onions begin to soften. Add the diced peppers and sauté just for few seconds.
Add chilli sauce and salt as per taste and finally add rice.
Mix rice with very lightly to heat through and garnish with spring onions.

Caramelised Onion Rice

What you will need:

1 tablespoon of oil
1 large onion
1 tablespoon of sugar
1 teaspoon of cinnamon
1 cup of Basmati Rice
1 1/2 cups of Water

What you will need to do:

Add oil to a large, non-stick pan and add the chopped onion, then the sugar. Stir and turn to low Cook on low for 20 minutes, stirring often, until the onions are sticky, clear and beginning to turn brown.
Add the cinnamon, stir and cook for a minute, then add the rice and water
Cover and cook for 15 minutes, until the rice is cooked, and water evaporated
If the rice is cooked, replace the lid and turn off the heat.
Allow the rice to sit in the pan steaming in its own heat for 10 minutes further

Pea and Mint Rice with Feta

What you will need:

2 cups of vegetable stock
cup of brown rice
1 1/2 cups of frozen peas
4 spring onions
¼ of a cup of crumbled feta cheese
Handful of fresh mint
Ground black pepper to taste

What you will need to do:

Finely chop the spring onions and the mint.
In a large saucepan bring vegetable stock to a rolling boil then add the rice and bring to a simmer. Cover and reduce the heat to low and cook for 4 minutes.
Stir in peas and return to a simmer. Cover once more and, simmer until the peas are hot and the rice has absorbed most of the liquid.
Remove from the heat and stir in scallions, feta, mint and pepper. Cover and let stand for 3 – 4 minutes before serving.

Asparagus Pea and Mint Rice Salad

<u>What you will need:</u>

1 cup of mixed basmati and wild rice
2 cups of water
2 shallots
Zest and juice of 1 lemon
4 tablespoons of sunflower oil
Handful of fresh mint
12 asparagus tips
1 cup of frozen peas

<u>What you will need to do:</u>

Cook the rice in salted water and then allow to cool. Finely dice the shallots and roughly shred the mint In a small bowl, mix together the shallots, lemon zest and juice, oil and mint, then stir into the rice.
Bring a large pan of lightly salted water to the boil. Add the asparagus and peas, and cook for 3-4 minutes until tender. Drain and refresh in a bowl of cold water. Drain the vegetables again and stir into the rice. Put into a serving dish and garnish with mint.

Fish and Seafood

Scotland is renowned for its abundance of fish. My wee granny most commonly cooked with herrings, salmon, trout, whiting, haddock, mackerel and cod. Many Scottish fish dishes are served with a traditional egg sauce.

Fish is low in saturated fat and low in the bad omega-6 fatty acids, high in protein and bursts with flavour. Oily fish such as mackerel and salmon are high in omega-3 fatty acids which are very good for the body.

Always ensure your fish is fresh by checking that the eyes are clear. If in doubt, place your fish in water and, if it floats, then it is fresh.

Some of these fish dish recipes date back to the 1800s and were popular during the 1900s and are still used in Scotland even today.

Please note that lard or dripping has been replaced by vegetable oil or butter.

Baked Cod

Serves 4

What you will need:

A cup of basic fish stock
4 cod loins
12 cherry tomatoes
2 tablespoons of flat leaf parsley
The juice of one lemon

What you will need to do:

Put the cod loins and the cherry tomatoes in an oven proof dish and cover with the fish stock. Add the lemon juice. Place in a preheated moderate oven and bake for twenty minutes.
Garnish with the parsley.

Cabbie Claw (1)

Serves 4-6

<u>What you will need</u>:

1lb cod fillets
1lb potatoes
2oz butter
1 dessertspoon of cornflour
Half a teaspoon of dried mustard
1 hard-boiled egg
3oz grated cheese
Half a pint of milk
Salt and pepper

<u>What you will need to do</u>:

Boil the potatoes until cooked then slice them
Put most of the milk, butter, salt and pepper into a frying pan and add the cod. Bring to a slow boil and simmer gently for 6 or 7 minutes or until the fish is cooked through.
Mix the cornflour with the remaining milk and add the mustard. Mix thoroughly and add to the pan.
Shake gently to mix through and continue shaking gently until the sauce thickens.
Turn out into a casserole dish.

Place the sliced potatoes on top, add the grated cheese and put in a pre-heated hot oven for 10 minutes.

Cabbie Claw (2)

Serves 4-6

What you will need:

200mls of basic fish stock
1lb cod fillets
Half a cup of curly leaf parsley
Quarter of an inch of grated horseradish
900g (1lb) potatoes
1 dessertspoon of cornflour

What you will need to do:

Boil the potatoes, cool and slice
Finely chop the parsley
Mix the cornflour with a little of the cold fish stock
Bring the remaining fish stock to the boil and reduce the heat to a gentle simmer. Add the cod and gently simmer for 5 minutes and then add the chopped parsley and the grated horseradish. Simmer for a further 5 minutes and then gently add the cornflour and thicken the stock by gently stirring (trying not to break up the cod.).
Turn out into a casserole dish and layer the potatoes on top.
Serve with egg sauce.

Traditional Whiting

Serves 4

What you will need:

2 cups of basic fish stock
8 whiting fillets
2 tablespoons of flour
3 knobs of butter
2 tablespoons of cream
2 tablespoons of chopped chives
Half a cup of chopped parsley

What you will need to do:

Ensure your fillets are dry and rub each of them with flour
Add the knobs of butter to a large frying pan, melt and add the fish and gently sauté them very slowly for 2 minutes. DO NOT brown them.
Ensure the chives and the parsley are very finely chopped and put in a bowl with the fish stock and mix thoroughly then add to the pan.
Bring to a gentle simmer and simmer for 2 or 3 minutes.
Try not to break them up when you lift them out. 2 fillets per portion

Curled Whiting
Serves 4

What you will need:

4 whole whiting with eyes removed
Half a cup of breadcrumbs
50g of melted butter
Salt and pepper
Third of a cup of chopped curly leaf parsley
Four lemon wedges

What you will need to do:

Curl each of the fish and put the tail through the eye socket.
Place in a greased tin and brush over the melted butter.
Season with the salt and pepper and sprinkle over with the breadcrumbs
Put in a preheated moderate oven and bake for 30 minutes
Garnish with the chopped parsley and the lemon wedges

Whiting Pudding

Serves 4

What you will need:

4 whole whiting
900g of potatoes (2lbs)
Half a pint (250mls) of milk
Salt and pepper
100g of butter

What you will need to do:

Boil the fish in the milk for 15 minutes
Boil the potatoes until cooked
Remove, debone and deskin
Mash the fish
Strain the milk and add 3 tablespoons to the cooked potatoes along with half of the butter. Mash and mix in the fish.
Mash the potato and fish mix to an oven proof dish and smooth out with a knife. Add the remaining butter in small dollops across the top.
Brown in a moderate oven.
Serve with egg sauce.

Traditional Herrings

Serves 4

What you will need:

8 fresh boned herring fillets (flattened carefully)
Salt and pepper
2 cups of oatmeal
Vegetable oil

What you will need to do:

Ensure the herring fillets are dry
Season with salt and pepper
Put oatmeal on a large plate and thoroughly coat each fillet with the oatmeal
Put vegetable oil in a large frying pan and heat until very hot
Add the herring and brown them until crisp on both sides
Lay on paper to drain the excess oil and serve immediately

Potted Herring
Serves 6

What you will need:

12 fresh boned herring fillets
Salt and pepper
12 black peppercorns
2 bay leaves
Half a cup of vinegar
Half a cup of water

What you will need to do:

Season each fillet with salt and pepper
Mix the half cup of vinegar with the half cup of water
Roll each fillet inside out starting from the tail end
Pack them side by side in a small pie dish and just cover with the vinegar and water mix
Add the 12 peppercorns and 2 bay leaves and bake in a preheated moderate oven

Crappit Heids (stuffed heads 1)

Serves 8

What you will need:

0.5 litres of basic fish stock
8 haddock heads
One cup of oatmeal
100g of butter
2 onions
One cup of white crab meat
2 anchovies
Chopped cooked yolk of 2 eggs
1 beaten egg
One cup of breadcrumbs
Salt and pepper

What you will need to do:

Chop and dice the onions and mix through the oatmeal. Add the anchovies, the crabmeat and the breadcrumbs and mix thoroughly.

Break up the butter and add. Bind the mixture with the beaten egg and gently fold in the chopped egg yolks.

Use the mixture to stuff the 8 haddock heads and place them on end on the bottom of a large buttered stew pan. Cover with the fish stock, bring to the boil and simmer for 30 minutes.

Crappit Heids (stuffed heads 2)

Serves 8

What you will need:

0.5 litres of basic fish stock
8 haddock heads
One cup of haddock livers
One cup of oatmeal
Half a cup of milk
Salt and pepper

What you will need to do:

Chop the livers and mix with the oatmeal. Bind with the milk. Season with salt and pepper.
Stuff the heads with the mixture and place the heads on end on the bottom of a large stew pot. Cover with the fish stock. Bring to the boil and simmer for 30 minutes.

Tatties and Herring

Serves 4

What you will need:

0.5 litres of basic fish stock
900g (2lbs) potatoes
8 salt herring fillets

What you will need to do:

Peel and dice the potatoes
Put in a large pot and cover with the fish stock.
Lay the salt herring fillets on top.
Bring to a slow boil and gently simmer on a very low heat for   minutes.

Spiced Salmon

Serves 4

<u>What you will need</u>:

4 salmon fillets
28g of salt
28g of black peppercorns
28g of cinnamon
One-pint (500mls) Vinegar
One pint of water

<u>What you will need to do</u>:

Mix the water and vinegar and add the salt, peppercorns and cinnamon. Add the salmon fillets and bring to the boil. Simmer for 10 minutes.
Remove the salmon and allow to cool then pack them in a deep dish and cover completely with the cooled cooking liquor. Cover so the dish is airtight. Serve with egg sauce.

Salmon Fritters

Serves 4

What you will need:

4 cooked salmon fillets
450g (1lb) of boiled potatoes
Yolk of one egg
4 hard-boiled eggs
2 tablespoons of cream
Vegetable oil
Salt and pepper

What you will need to do:

Mash the boiled potatoes and mix in the egg yolk and the cream. Season with salt and pepper.
Flake the cooked salmon fillets through the mashed potatoes and mix thoroughly.
Mold into small fritters and fry in vegetable oil until golden on both sides.
Each portion to be served with a quartered hard-boiled egg.

Friar's Trout in Sauce

Serves 4

What you will need:

Half a litre of basic fish stock
4 cleaned and gutted whole trout
2 onions
4 cloves
4 teaspoons of black peppercorns
2 teaspoons of salt
2 glasses of white wine
4 anchovies
Juice of 1 lemon
One teaspoon of cayenne pepper
1 dessertspoon of cornflour
100g butter

What you will need to do:

Mix the peppercorns, salt and cayenne pepper together and divide into 4 portions. Use one portion per trout and rub the mix inside the belly of the fish. Place the fish in a stew pan and cover with the stock. Chop and dice the onions and add to the pot. Add the 4 cloves.

Bring to the boil and gently simmer for 5 minutes and then add the 2 glasses of wine and the 4 anchovies. Add the lemon juice.

Gently simmer for 20 minutes then gently remove the trout and place in a casserole dish.

Thicken the stock with cornflour and add the butter. Pour the stock over the trout and serve hot.

Potted Salmon

Serves 4

<u>What you will need</u>:

4 fillets of salmon
The juice and zest of 1 lemon
1 teaspoon of chopped dill
1 teaspoon of chopped flat parsley
1 teaspoon of cayenne pepper
200g of unsalted butter
Salt and pepper

<u>What you will need to do</u>:

Flake the salmon fillets and put in a bowl.
Add the lemon juice and zest, the dill and the parsley and mix. Taste and add salt and pepper to season…
Pour in three quarters of the melted butter and mix thoroughly.
Taste again and add more seasoning if required.
Divide the salmon mix between 4 teacups and smooth the tops before brushing on the remaining butter.
Chill in the fridge for 2 hours before serving.
Serve with toasted bread.

Leek and Mackerel Patties

Serves 4

What you will need:

450g (1lb) potatoes
2 leeks
1 tablespoon of capers
4 mackerel fillets
100g of butter
Half a cup of milk
Salt and pepper
Vegetable oil

What you will need to do:

Boil the potatoes in salted water and mash with the butter
Cut the leeks up very small and poach to soften in the milk and season with the salt and pepper.
Add the mackerel to the milk and leeks and continue poaching until the fish is cooked through. When cooked, drain then flake the mackerel with a fork and add to the mashed potatoes. Mix thoroughly and make into small patties.
Fry the patties in the vegetable oil until golden on both sides.
Serve with egg sauce.

Crispy Skinned Mackerel

Serves 4

<u>What you will need</u>:

4 butterflied mackerel skin on
1 spring onion
1 lemon
Salt and pepper

<u>What you will need to do</u>:

Heat a frying pan until piping hot and add the mackerel skin down. Season with salt and pepper and grate the zest of the lemon over it. Fry until the skin side is dark brown – pressing down with a fish slice (for about 3 minutes) then flip over and fry for a few seconds on the other side.
Trim and finely slice the spring onions and sprinkle over the cooked fish.
Serve with buttered toast.

Crappit Cod (stuffed cod)

Serves 6-8

What you will need:

Half a litre of basic fish stock
One whole cod, cleaned, descaled and gutted
The meat from one cooked crab
4 anchovies
2 cooked egg yolks
2 eggs
1 cup of oatmeal
100g of butter
Half a cup of flat leaf parsley

What you will need to do:

Mix the crab meat, the anchovies, the oatmeal, the egg yolks, the butter and the parsley thoroughly together and stuff it into the belly of the cod.
Put the cod in a fish bath and cover with the fish stock. Cover and bake in a moderate oven for one hour.
Add additional seasoning if required.
Serve with egg sauce.

John Dory with Cockles, Spinach and Egg Sauce

Serves 6

What you will need:

6 John Dory fillets
300g of cockles
2 tablespoons of butter
300g of baby spinach
Salt and pepper
2 tablespoons of olive oil

What you will need to do:

Rub the John Dory in half of the olive oil and season with the salt and pepper then steam the fish for approximately 10 minutes
Cook the cockles in seasoned boiling water that has had the remaining olive oil added until the shells all open (2 or 3 minutes will do)
Sauté the spinach in butter (2 minutes should do it)
Serve the fish on top of the spinach. Drain the cockles and pour over the fish.
Serve with egg sauce.

Lobster and Fennel Salad

What you will need:

1 lobster (live)
4 baby fennel bulbs
1 clove of garlic
100mls of white wine
2 tablespoons of butter
4 spring onions
1 teaspoon of black peppercorns
salt

What you need to do:

Bring a large pot of water to the boil and add the wine, garlic, peppercorns and whole lobster. Boil for 8 minutes
Meantime, halve the fennel bulbs and fry in the butter until soft
Remove the lobster and, when cool, remove the meat – leaving it as intact as possible, then slice and divide into 4 portions
Finely dice the spring onions
Serve the lobster on top of the fennel and garnish with the spring onions

Smoked Mackerel Pate

Prepare in advance

What you will need:

4 smoked mackerel fillets
4 tablespoons of creamed cheese
Quarter of a red onion
1 teaspoon of lemon juice
1 teaspoon of butter
1 teaspoon of fine brandy
Salt and pepper

What you need to do:

Finely mince the red onion

Thoroughly mix and combine the cream cheese, butter, onion, lemon juice and brandy. Season with salt and pepper.

Flake the smoked mackerel through the mix and spoon into 4 ramekins. Cover with cling-film and put in the fridge for at least 4 hours.

Crab cakes

<u>What you will need:</u>

600g of cooked, flaked crab meat
400g of potatoes
2 egg
40g of plain flour
2 tablespoons of butter
100g of fresh breadcrumbs
Salt and pepper
1 teaspoon of lemon juice

<u>What you need to do:</u>

Peel and boil the potatoes in salted water, then drain and mash with one tablespoon of the butter. Allow to thoroughly cool, then mix through the flaked crab meat and the lemon juice. Season to taste with the salt and pepper
Beat the eggs. Shape the potato mixture into 8 portions, dip in the egg, flatten into cakes and coat in the breadcrumbs.
Fry the potato cakes in the remaining butter until golden brown on both sides

Tiger Prawns with Creamy Whisky Sauce

What you will need:

12 tiger prawns, de-shelled and de-veined
500ml of double cream
2 teaspoons of wholegrain mustard
1 tablespoon of Dijon mustard
2 teaspoons of whisky
sea salt and freshly ground white pepper
1 tablespoon of chopped fresh chives
1 tablespoon of lemon juice
1 tablespoon of butter
Salt and pepper

What you will need to do:

Add the cream to a saucepan and heat through gently then add the 2 mustards and the whisky. Stir and increase the heat to a simmer. Simmer for a couple of minutes then remove from the heat. Add the chopped chives and the lemon juice and season with the salt and pepper.

Meantime butterfly the tiger prawns and fry gently in the butter until cooked – being careful not to overcook.

Serve 3 per portion topped with the whisky sauce.

Sea Bass and Seafood Supper

What you will need:

4 sea bass fillets
8 large raw prawns
8 mussels
2 tablespoons of olive oil
1 fennel bulb
1 squid around 250g
2 garlic cloves
½ red chilli
Bunch of basil
Can of chopped tomatoes
1 cup of white wine
salt and pepper to taste

What you will need to do:

Half and slice the fennel bulb and keep the fronds separate to garnish
Slice the garlic and finely chop the chili
Roughly chop the basil leaves and keep the stalks separate
Clean the squid and cut into rings

Heat the oil in a large saucepan with a tight-fitting lid, then add the fennel, garlic and chilli. Fry until softened, then add the squid, basil stalks, tomatoes and wine. Simmer over a low heat for 35 mins until the squid is tender and the sauce has thickened slightly, then season.

Scatter the mussels and prawns over the sauce, lay the sea bass fillets on top, cover, turn up the heat and cook hard for 5 mins. Serve scattered with the basil leaves and fennel fronts

Stir Fried Prawns with Peppers and Spinach

What will you will need:

3 tablespoons of sunflower oil
2 garlic cloves
1 small red pepper
200g pack raw peeled tiger prawn
tablespoons of soy sauce
2 handfuls of baby spinach leaves

What you will need to do:

Finely slice the garlic
Core and de-seed the pepper and slice
Heat a wok and add the sunflower oil and, then the garlic slices. Stir-fry until they start to turn golden, then using a slotted spoon, spoon onto kitchen paper to drain.
Toss in the pepper and stir-fry for 1 min or so until softened, then scoop out and set aside.
Add the remaining tbsp oil. Heat, then toss in the prawns and stir-fry for another 2-3 mins until cooked and beginning to brown. Add the sauce.
Throw in the spinach and stir-fry until it begins to wilt. Return the peppers and crisp garlic to the wok, then serve immediately.

Printed in Great Britain
by Amazon